T0292792

Phoenix Leadership for Business

An Executive's Strategy for Relevance and Resilience

Phoenix Leadership for Business

An Executive's Strategy for Relevance and Resilience

By
Val Gokenbach, DM, RN, MBA, RWJF, NEA-BC
Foreword by Dr. Jean Ann Larson, FACHE, LFHIMSS, FIISE, OCC

Routledge
Taylor & Francis Group

A PRODUCTIVITY PRESS BOOK

First edition published in 2019
by Routledge/Productivity Press
711 Third Avenue, New York, NY 10017, USA
2 Park Square, Milton Park, Abingdon, Oxon OX14 4RN, UK

© 2019 by Val Gokenbach
Routledge/Productivity Press is an imprint of Taylor & Francis Group, an Informa business

No claim to original U.S. Government works

Printed on acid-free paper

International Standard Book Number-13: 978-1-138-54261-7 (Hardback)

Library of Congress Cataloging-in-Publication Data

Names: Gokenbach, Valentina, author.
Title: Phoenix leadership for business : an executive's strategy for
relevance and resilience / Valentina Gokenbach.
Description: 1 Edition. | New York : Taylor & Francis, [2019] | Includes
bibliographical references and index.
Identifiers: LCCN 2018031771 (print) | LCCN 2018035045 (ebook) | ISBN
9781351008327 (e-Book) | ISBN 9781138542617 (hardback : alk. paper)
Subjects: LCSH: Leadership. | Interpersonal relations. | Self-confidence. | Personnel management.
Classification: LCC HD57.7 (ebook) | LCC HD57.7 .G645 2019 (print) | DDC 658.4/092–dc23
LC record available at https://lccn.loc.gov/2018031771

Visit the Taylor & Francis Web site at
http://www.taylorandfrancis.com

No successful leader excels on their own, but rather with the support and coaching of caring mentors. I have had many mentors throughout my career who have helped me grow and succeed. I dedicate this book to all of my amazing mentors. I love and appreciate you all for helping me get to where I am now.

Contents

Foreword

Being a leader of any enterprise is more challenging than ever before. Just when we think we have it all figured out, new challenges present themselves and we are suddenly faced with having to reinvent ourselves as leaders. Dr. Val Gokenbach's book, *Phoenix Leadership for Business An Executive's Strategy for Relevance and Resilience*, offers a life line to leaders seeking inspiration and innovative approaches as they face an ever-increasing complex environment.

I first met Val when I was working as a process engineer in a large southeast Michigan-based health system in charge of leading the organization's process improvement efforts. The organization had almost 16,000 employees at the time, and I was beginning to feel a bit in over my head. Val arrived as a new leader and her can-do attitude felt like a breath of fresh air. When I told her what I was trying to accomplish, she was the first person to encourage me and have faith in my ability to deliver on what I was trying to do; all the while asking pointed and challenging questions that allowed me to think out loud and share concerns and strategies with a broader audience.

It has been many years since Val and I first worked together, but she served as a mentor, colleague and friend as we both rose through the organization and began work on our doctorates sharing a passion for leadership and a keen appreciation of its impact upon organizational culture and the people who devote themselves tirelessly to the practice of being leaders. We also moved away to other organizations and opportunities, but we've always stayed in touch and I've admired her continued success from afar.

I feel honored to write this foreword for Val's book because she is a leader who lives and leads authentically and passionately. I have observed her ability to lead and inspire others even through the very challenging times of one of the most serious economic downturns in our recent history.

She has faith in her colleagues and leads them to do more than they ever think they are capable of doing. After years of studying leadership, organizational change and observing many leaders – some good, some bad – Val is one of the best leaders I have seen who can live her values and achieve stellar results while inspiring excellence in others.

When I read about other's ideas about leadership – or any other topic for that matter – I want to know about the author as a person. Do they have not only the not only the educational credentials but do they also have valuable lived experience that I can learn from? Have they been where I want to go and do they have practical wisdom to write about how I might approach my challenges? You will find that Val describes leadership and organizational theory very succinctly and applies them clearly and brilliantly to healthcare. Kurt Lewin, who Val quotes in the book, once said, "there is nothing so practical as a good theory." And this is true throughout the book as Val weaves theory with her own experience, stories and approaches to everyday leadership challenges.

So, whether you are an experienced leader or an emerging leader, you will find this book to be of value to you as you come into your own as an effective leader. This book takes you from leadership theory to practical application of that theory. If you are a new leader, the book will ground you in classic leadership theory. And, if you are an experienced leader, Val provides a great overview and refresher course in leadership and organizational theory. She also generously shares her extensive personal and professional experience based upon her more than 30 years as a senior leader and through compelling personal and professional stories. Most importantly, each chapter concludes with a chance for you to reflect upon and apply the concepts to your professional situation and setting.

Dr. Val Gokenbach's *Phoenix Leadership for Business An Executive's Strategy for Relevance and Resilience* describes the attributes of a Phoenix Leader that we can all aspire to and intentionally develop. Through the metaphor of the Phoenix, each attribute is covered in depth giving you the awareness and skills to build that attribute in yourself as a leader. The attributes include:

- Strong sense of self
- Effective interpersonal relationships
- Ability to build an empowered workforce
- Innovation
- Resilience

Phoenix Leadership will engage you whatever your background and help you reinvent yourself as a leader to meet the ongoing challenges in your organization. Reading it is like inviting a wise consultant in to be your trusted advisor, coach and friend as Val has been to me and many other leaders. She shares her journey of holistic personal and professional leadership helping you lead yourself and your organization. I know you are going to find this book as practical and valuable as I have.

Best wishes on your leadership development journey,

Dr. Jean Ann Larson, FACHE, LFHIMSS, FIISE, OCC
Chief Leadership Development Officer, University of Alabama at Birmingham Health System and School of Medicine, CEO of Jean Ann Larson and Associates, a boutique Leadership Development Consultancy Practice National speaker and author of several books Author of *Organizational and Process Reengineering: Approaches for Healthcare Transformation*, winner of the Healthcare Information and Management Systems Society 2015 Book of the Year Award

Author

Dr. Val Gokenbach has a true passion for leadership and has been in administrative positions for more than 30 years. She currently is the vice president and chief nursing officer for Baylor Scott and White Health and the owner of Dr. Val Leading Leaders Consulting Group, dedicated to improving the quality of leadership in organizations. As a senior executive, she has managed an expansive span of responsibility, which included nursing and several support departments, such as radiology, respiratory therapy, radiation oncology, nuclear medicine, oncology services, neurodiagnostic services, employee health, integrative medicine, schools of allied health, patient service departments and emergency services. Her greatest accomplishment has been leading the nursing team to the receipt of the prestigious Magnet accreditation awarded on January 14, 2004, for nursing and organizational excellence and reaccreditation in 2008.

Val has also been involved in several community initiatives and served as the creator of Safety City USA, the first freestanding, nonprofit interactive learning facility for the community, dedicated to the reduction of pediatric trauma, and Nurses 4 Detroit, a foundation for philanthropic nurses in the southeast Michigan area. Currently, she is an independent consultant in the areas of organizational structure and leadership growth and development. She also served as the medical administrator for Mitch Albom Charities, where she ran the SAY Detroit Family Health Center, dedicated to the care of the homeless and uninsured women and children, and the Have Faith Mission, an orphanage in Haiti.

She also lectures on leadership topics and is active on several advisory and leadership boards throughout the country. A well-known author, she released her own wellness book, *Tap Dancing through Life: Seven Steps to Finding Your Rhythms and the Life of Your Dreams*. She is also featured in *Chicken Soup for the Nurse's Soul: A Second Dose* and *Nurse Executive: The Four Principles of Management* from Springer Publishing.

She possesses a doctoral degree in management (DM) and organizational leadership, a master of business administration (MBA) and a bachelor of science in nursing (BSN), and she is a Robert Wood Johnson Executive Nurse Fellow, was a Magnet commissioner for the American Nurses Credentialing Center and was an alumnus for Leadership America.

Chapter 1

Status of Organizational Leadership in the United States

Your present circumstances don't determine where you can go;
they merely determine where you start.

Nido R. Qubein

Leadership: An Awesome Responsibility

I began my leadership career in healthcare when I was appointed manager
of an intensive care unit 1 year after my graduation from nursing school. I
was promoted because my director said that I had leadership abilities and
I was the best clinical nurse. As I was planning my next move up the ladder of leadership, I decided that I would go back to school for my master
of business administration (MBA). At that time, most of the chief executive
officers (CEOs) and chief financial officers (CFOs) were MBAs. Degrees in
healthcare administration were just emerging, and I felt that if I wanted to
speak the language of the leaders, I needed the same educational background that they had.

The MBA program was very difficult but fascinating to me, but what was
especially valuable to me was that I was attending with students from a
variety of industries, such as manufacturing, service and sales. This provided

a wealth of diverse learning experiences that taught me to think in different ways. In my studies on quality improvement, focusing on the works of Edwards Deming and others, I learned the concept of the widget. A widget is nothing more than a word to apply to any unit of production in the world of manufacturing. When Deming and others spoke of zero defects, it was to prevent financial loss due to the improper manufacturing of whatever widget that was in production. These defective parts, if used, can lead to national recalls, safety concerns for consumers and the potential for legal exposures in the event of an injury.

What was illuminating for me at the time was the notion that in healthcare, our unit of production, or our widget, is the patient. The profound difference, however, is that a patient, unlike an inanimate widget, is far more complex and has a high degree of variability, making it very difficult for those of us in healthcare to develop processes that meet the specific needs of all patients. Other compounding complexities of patient care include understanding and dealing with emotions, knowledge base, culture, diversities, family concerns, finances, language differences and other unique attributes of the particular individual. In other words, the complexity and unpredictability of the human being makes the delivery of healthcare very challenging. If a company produces a batch of widgets that cannot be used and is therefore discarded, there is a financial loss to the organization for product, resources and time. If there is a breech in the delivery of healthcare, it can result in the injury or death of a patient, which is a tremendous responsibility for healthcare providers. As healthcare executives, we must continue to strive for zero defects, which in our industry translates to the highest degree of quality and safety. Unfortunately, in my career I have worked with individuals that looked upon patients as widgets, and even in the care area observed staff that focused on tasks while forgetting the emotional needs of the patient. These concepts can apply also to service organizations that have high personal touch points with consumers and other businesses. It is critical that all organizations strive for continued quality and safety in their products and services. To illustrate this point, I like to use the concept of a plane crash that creates a visual for why quality and safety are so important.

Concept of a Plane Crash

The news of a plane crash is always troubling to hear. We are impacted by the massive loss of life, especially if the incident involves a large plane.

We feel for the families that are left behind and for what their lives will be like without their loved ones. The reality is that every injury or death for a patient secondary to medical error *is* a plane crash for that patient and family, yet the emotional impact to us does not seem to be the same, but it should be. A similar analogy can be made in any business. Products need to be safe for the consumer; manufacturing facilities need to be safe for workers. Any breach in quality and safety can kill or injure people—a plane crash for them and their families.

The statistical comparison is profound. The Aviation Safety Network (ASN) is one of the organizations that are responsible for tracking statistics on the safety of aviation. In 2014, the ASN reported 761 deaths in 12 commercial aviation accidents. In 2015, the number was much less, at 265 deaths. The year 2015 was recognized as the safest in aviation. This translates to 0.24 deaths per 1 million departures.

The Institute of Medicine (IOM), in their report *To Err Is Human*, reported that 98,000 patients die every year secondary to mistakes in hospitals. The inspector general for Health and Human Services in 2010 reported that in Medicare patients alone, the number of injury or death incidents was 180,000. The last report from the *Journal of Patient Safety* anticipates that the numbers may be grossly understated and could be as high as 210,000–440,000. It is much safer to fly than it is to seek healthcare. This information underscores the need for effective leadership in healthcare, as well as what an awesome responsibility healthcare leaders bear.

The U.S. Department of Labor (2016) has shown an increase in employee deaths from 2013 to 2017 despite regulation and safety requirements. The employee injury rate in 2017 per 100 full-time workers was a staggering 7.7. The U.S. Consumer Product and Safety Commission (2017) reports staggering rates of injury and death in consumers in a multitude of product categories. Every one of these represents a plane crash for the individual and their families.

Leadership Is the Answer to Quality, Safety and Effectiveness

The important concepts of quality, safety and effectiveness in organizations will not be realized without the engagement and effective leadership of staff, who at the point of service make magic happen. The literature strongly suggests that engaged staff are more focused at work and provide

safer and higher-quality work (Gallup, 2016b). Unfortunately, the environment in many organizations does not support a nurturing and enjoyable
work environment. Human resource research has repeatedly identified that
staff disengagement and turnover is a result of the employee's desire to leave
their manager, and very little turnover is for other reasons, such as moving,
money or promotions. Gallup's report on the state of the American workforce in 2013 identified that most employees across the country are dissatis-
fied with their workplace. They published that

■ Eighteen percent of the workforce is actively disengaged or disgruntled.
■ Fifty-two percent of employees are identified as "present" but not
engaged.
■ Thirty percent of the employees are identified as engaged and inspired
by their work and their leaders.

This represents a tremendous dearth of leadership skill in all industries. If
we translate this into organizations alone, a staggering 70% of our employee
base is not working at their capacity, leading to a loss of productivity. The
report further explains that as much as $550 billion in productivity is lost
due to the 18% that are disengaged. Compound this over time and the
effect on profitability is staggering. It means that quality and safety could be
greatly impacted as well when employees are not present.

A good friend of mine said that the flavor of the sundae always starts at
the top. My experience as a healthcare executive and my experiences in the
consulting arena have proven this to be true. No organization is going to be
successful unless the leaders are effective. In my mind, leadership is a science with a body of theories and research that, when studied and applied,
improve the chance of organizational success. One of our challenges is
that we do not necessarily promote capable leaders. Especially in the clinical areas, such as medicine and nursing, there is the tendency to promote
the best clinicians, thinking that the ability to be a great clinician automatically transfers to the likelihood that they will be an effective leader. I have
seen practices in other industries where individuals move into the next-level
position due to an opening despite leadership capabilities—when they have
"paid their dues." We compound this problem by not providing the appropriate leadership education and development. This is due to the lack of insight
into the importance of leadership development on the part of the organization. Focusing on leadership development is one of the key elements to
organizational success, but in my experience, it is one of the vital strategies

easily sidelined with budgetary constraints or other organizational priorities. Especially in times of organizational challenges, leadership development is exactly what is needed.

Are Leaders Born or Made?

As I was growing up, my mother used to tell me that I was a natural-born leader because I ruled the neighborhood kids and always told them what to do, and what was amazing to her was that they listened to me. My perspective on this had nothing to do with my effective leadership skills but rather the fact that I wanted to keep them away from my stuff. To that end, I was the one who organized play based on my desires. What was interesting is that my friends were always accepting of my recommendations. For years, leadership and behavioral theorists have been debating the question of whether leaders are born or made. The research now suggests that leaders are not born but can be made and developed with appropriate programs that focus on teaching, mentoring and learning. Bernard Bass (2008) had identified several characteristics inherent in successful leaders but also believed that these can be observed, and many of them acquired over time. Research published in *Psychology Today* reported that characteristics of successful leaders include assertiveness, risk-taking, extraversion, emotional intelligence and social intelligence (Arvey et al., 2006). Arvey et al. also believed that these characteristics can be studied and acquired over time with the right programs and guidance.

Difference between Leadership and Management

Stephen Covey identified the difference between leadership and management when he stated, "Effective leadership is putting first things first. Effective management is discipline, carrying it out." More simply put, management is *doing* and leading is *inspiring*. John Kotter described that there is a profound difference between managing and leading despite the fact that the terms are oftentimes used interchangeably. This is important to note. Kotter further described the function of management as one of planning, goal setting, and budgeting, staffing and other operational tasks. What is important to realize is that when the operational tasks are completed, they needed to be executed in a successful and effective way. Success will not be achieved unless the leader can inspire the staff to engage in the plans and be involved in the successful execution. There are many examples of people that I have worked with that were very good at the operational planning but struggled with execution. Not all good managers are leaders, but there is a greater likelihood that good leaders will be good managers (Kotter, 2002).

Evolution of Leadership Theory

In order to better understand modern leadership theories, it is important to look over the evolution of leadership over time. This reflection of the past sets the stage for the transformation of leadership theories over the years. Our focus begins with the Industrial Revolution.

Industrial Revolution

The Industrial Revolution began following the end of the Civil War, with the introduction of industry, manufacturing and growth of companies providing goods and services to local consumers. Prior to the Industrial Revolution, the United States was primarily agricultural. Newly created technologies, such as the cotton gin and steam engines, further advanced industry growth. Manpower was now needed to work in the factories and run the new machines, which led to the hiring of employees in exchange for wages.

The rapidly increasing demands for goods increased production pressure and the need to extend hours in the factories. This demand resulted in longer shifts, unbearable heat and an absence of safety measures, oftentimes resulting in injury and death to workers. Employees were viewed as a means to an end, with little attention paid to their human value. Children were also exploited, and there were no labor laws to protect any of the workers. Leadership adopted an autocratic approach, with all decisions made by the leaders, who pushed their workers to produce despite the conditions and minimal wages.

In the early 1950s, American workers began to rebel against their employers, creating bargaining units and unions to use collective power and pressure through work stoppage and strikes. These formalized unions provided a forum for the workers to be heard and force changes in leadership approaches. These pressures on leadership gave rise to the human resource era of leadership.

Human Resource Era

The United States continues to reside in the human resource era, character-ized by an appreciation of workers for their contribution to the success of an organization. This was also coupled with competitive pay and benefit packages, including vacation and sick time, healthcare and tuition reimburse-ment. Workplace satisfaction now is a key driver for employees seeking new jobs. The draw of nurses to Magnet hospitals is an example of such attrac-tion to organizations that appreciate their staff. There are still examples of autocratic approaches to leadership, but the healthcare industry continues to move away from this type of leadership. There are a variety of leader-ship approaches that can be applied to the right work environment or circumstance.

Leadership Approaches

In order for leaders to apply the appropriate leadership strategy, it is impor-tant to understand some of the common theories, the category of worker that these approaches are more effective with and the situations in which to apply them. Bass (1990) has identified the following as common approaches.

Autocratic/Authoritarian

Lewin et al. conducted the first research on this approach to leadership in 1939. The work was updated by Kendra Cherry in 2016. They characterized this approach to leadership as one of total, individual control by the leader, with no advice from others or followers, thus providing authoritarian control over a group. They identified that the application of this approach is neces-sary when there is a need for strong leadership or in crisis situations when it is imperative to make quick, decisive choices. Disasters and emergency situations are good examples of when this approach is needed and most effective.

There are, however, several downsides to this type of leadership if applied to all scenarios over time. It is easy to abuse this power, causing resentment among the employees secondary to the controlling and dictato-rial tone of the leader. Also, since the leader in this situation is making all the decisions based on their thoughts and experiences, it is easy for them to lack creative and innovative thoughts due to this insulation. Highly educated and capable healthcare workers require the ability to grow and contribute in their work environment, so this type of leadership is stifling to them, rendering it not appropriate for a professional workforce.

Democratic/Egalitarian

Democratic leadership is one of the participatory approaches that allows for the staff to take a more active role in decision-making. Research has identified this approach to leadership as one of the most effective, leading to higher productivity, increased innovation, strong contributions from staff and improved engagement and morale (Cherry, 2016a). Despite the positive research on democratic leadership, there are some potential downsides as well. This approach works in situations where the employees are skilled and well educated, which makes it appropriate for the healthcare setting. If the leader is not effective and the employees are not prepared to contribute effectively to decision-making, there could be confusion and lack of direction. Last, the term *democratic leadership* does not necessarily mean that the staff have ultimate control over the decisions, but that they can contribute suggestions and their knowledge to those decisions. It is important that the staff does not misunderstand the expectations. It is critically important, however, that the leader listens to their contributions.

Transactional

Transactional leadership was first described by Max Webber in 1947 as a highly structured approach to leadership whereby the leader gives something to the follower in exchange for something the leader needs. This could be reward or punishment. Bass (2008) further studied transactional leadership and identified the following tenets:

- Transactions are rewards contingent on the process of setting clear expectations and workers meeting them.
- Transactional leadership is passive, whereby the manager does not interfere with the workers or the workflow unless an issue arises.
- Transactional leadership is not a participative approach.

There are examples of transactional leadership as a component in all organizations. Employees get paid for their work and are rewarded via evaluations and recognition. In my experience, another example of a transaction is the payment of overtime, double time or premium pay during times of staffing crisis. Once this type of transaction is made, it is difficult to stop the process. I have had staff refuse to work overtime unless they receive premium pay, and many of my colleagues have had the same experience. This phenomenon is one of the drawbacks to transactional leadership as it does not engender loyalty in the staff, but rather the focus is on whether there is an acceptable reward. In the event that the leader needs to utilize such a system, the program needs to be well managed and the expectations of what constitutes a crisis need to be understood.

Contingency Theory

Another transactional approach to leadership is that of contingency theory, pioneered by Fred Fiedler in 1967. Fiedler identified two focuses of the contingency leader, one focused on the staff and the other on the situation. He proposed that leaders need to deal with various staff differently contingent on their knowledge base or expertise. For instance, highly skilled employees may have the latitude to function independently while the less skilled employees need more direction. He also believed that the situation can also dictate the leadership approach. In times of crisis, a more autocratic approach may be used or there may be times when participation of the staff is required. One of the major drawbacks of contingency theory is the potential loss of consistency of behavior of the leader, leading to confusion or distress among the staff (Bass, 2008).

Followership

Followership in leadership theory is not a new concept. It was first studied by Mary Parker Follett in 1933. Parker believed that the understanding of the followers and their needs is a skill that effective leaders need to have. Most studies, however, focused on leaders and their characteristics, with little focus on those who follow those leaders (Thach et al., 2006). Parker also believed that it is the followers that need to be willing, giving consent to the leader for what is expected of them. Depree (1992) supported the notion that leaders can only accomplish what they need to accomplish based on permission from the followers. In my experience, I also believe that the understanding of the characteristics of the staff is an important leadership skill and leaders will not be effective if they do not know how to unlock the hearts and minds of the staff. Unlocking their hearts is what will move them to success.

Servant

"The servant leader is servant first—it begins with the natural feeling that one wants to serve, to serve first" (Greenleaf, 1970). Greenleaf believed that the conscious choice of desiring to serve is what calls us to leadership. The servant leader makes sure that the staff is their highest priority and their needs are met before the leader's. They also want to touch the lives of those around them so that they grow and flourish in the environment. The servant leader also shares power with the staff, which helps them feel empowered, increasing the likelihood that they can function at their best. The reverse of this servant leader is leader servant, who places their needs, goals and desires before others. The latter is far from effective.

Coaching

My 8-year-old granddaughter plays on a very good baseball team and has won several trophies in the past 2 years. What is very fun is that they can all pick a "walk-up" song that they play on speakers when they come to the plate. After reviewing several appropriate songs, Abby selected "Put Me in Coach" by John Fogerty. The chorus is

> Oh, put me in, Coach—I'm ready to play today;
> Put me in, Coach—I'm ready to play today;
> Look at me, I can be Centerfield.

John Fogerty (1985)

With regard to the coaching approach to leadership, we want to inspire the staff to want to engage and be ready to play. Daniel Goldman (2013) described the unique approach to coaching in leadership as the ability of the leader to do more than simply lead the team to success, but to help employees identify their unique set of strengths and weaknesses and to align them with the roles that they play, as well as tie that to their personal growth aspirations. This approach is characterized by a commitment on the part of the leader to provide ongoing feedback and instruction. Employees that work for effective coach leaders feel that they are cared for and nurtured and are continually challenged to be their best. Unfortunately, production pressures on leaders, especially during turbulent times, such as those we are facing in healthcare, make it difficult for leaders to make a wholesale commitment to coaching, despite the effectiveness of coaching on morale and productivity, so coaching as a leadership approach is underutilized. The issue with this approach is a question of time and the leader's availability.

Transformational

With regard to leadership approaches, I saved the best for last. Bass (1990) described transformational leadership as the sharing of governance by the leader and the followers, resulting in the transformation of the leader, the staff and the organization. This is due to an increase in engagement secondary to the concept of empowerment. Dvir et al. (2002) studied the impact of transformational leadership on organizational effectiveness. They identified that the transformational approach to leadership is recognized as the most effective approach to use with professional staff that are independent in their practice based on their education and critical thinking abilities.

James Hillman (1996) described the acorn theory as the belief that all people are born like an acorn, inherently gifted with all they need to grow and thrive in this world. If properly supported, individuals will make the right appropriate choices in life utilizing this innate and perfect knowledge. The acorn grows into a beautiful oak tree without any outside direction.

Like the acorn, our talents are inherent. This is an empowering concept when the leader respects the innate wisdom of the staff. When the staff are empowered, they feel that they have input into their work environment and feel committed to their organization. The staff are also the individuals with the most perfect knowledge about what is going on at the point of service. I have always supported the notion that the farther a leader moves away from the point of service, the less right they have to make decisions about processes at the point of service. This distance cannot keep up with changes to processes that change over time.

The American Nurses Credentialing Center (ANCC), through the coveted Magnet designation, identifies transformational leadership as one of the major forces for the success of organizations increasing staff engagement, quality and improvement. Clavelle et al. (2012) described their study, which identifies the leadership practices of Magnet chief nursing officers (CNOs). They studied outcomes of organizations led by transformational nursing leaders and suggest that there is an integral connection to quality and safety in Magnet organizations. They also identified that one of the behaviors of the CNOs was to enable the staff to act in the clinical environment to improve care as well as the work environment. Aiken et al. (2009) in their studies also found the same correlation.

Magnet designation focuses on the quality of nursing in an organization, but the reality is that it is the ability of the nursing organization to collaborate with all departments that achieves this high level of success. If transformational leadership is effective with nursing, it stands to reason that this approach to leadership will also be effective with the multitude of other professionals in the healthcare environment. We see the same approach in organizations that have achieved the coveted Baldrige Award. Both of these designations are built on the solid foundation of effective leadership.

Organizational and Personal Effects of Ineffective Leadership

There is no debate that ineffective leadership impacts the organization as well as personal achievements and promotion of the leader. The biggest impact to the organization in cases of poor leadership is the negative effects on the staff. Human resource research suggests that the number one reason employees leave their organization is because of their inability to work with their leaders. This results in what I call the employee death spiral, whereby employees begin to leave the organization, causing vacancies and increased pressure on the remaining staff. The staff may be expected to work overtime to cover, or in some cases, contract labor is hired to replace the vacancies at a higher cost. Working excessive overtime leads to fatigue and further decrease of morale. Staff may not feel appreciated, so they also begin to leave. Once the exodus begins, there is a lack of hope on the part of the staff, so more people begin to leave, further increasing the number of vacancies. It may be difficult to recruit staff to the area since the reputation of the leader and the working conditions are generally known throughout the organization. This is also a tremendous financial burden on the organization, with these areas of high turnover consistently running over their manpower budgets.

It is also my experience that when contract labor utilization is high, there is the potential for a decrease in quality and service since agency nurses tend to be transient and not generally committed to the unit. There is also a perception on the part of the staff that agencies are paid at a much higher rate than they are. It is true that the cost of agency personnel is higher, but the differential is for the service and not necessarily paid to the staff. I have always worked to eliminate contract labor and have been very successful with that over the years. There are some consistent issues that are observed in ineffective leaders. We will be discussing them in greater detail later on in the book, but to set the context, here are some common causes of ineffective leadership.

Causes of Ineffective Leadership

Over my almost 40-year career in healthcare as an executive leader, consultant and educator, I have had the privilege to teach, coach and mentor many leaders, both emerging and experienced. As a consultant, I have had the opportunity to work with leaders to improve leadership practices for their whole organization. What I have observed as common causes of ineffective leadership are the following.

Inexperience

We touched on this briefly before when we spoke of the importance of leadership training that oftentimes is not available in the organization. Inexperienced leaders do not know what they do not know, so oftentimes, without any leadership training, new leaders may use trial and error as an approach to what works rather than proven theories.

Lack of Knowledge of Self

An effective leader has a high degree of awareness as to who they are as a person and what type of responses they have to certain situations. This also translates to a high degree of emotional and social intelligence. There are many types of evaluations available to use to begin to understand yourself, but it is also about understanding personal values, passions and future goals. We will be delving into these concepts later in the book.

Complacency

"If it's not broke, don't fix it" is never an effective leadership strategy. I have witnessed complacency in situations where the leader has been there for an extended period of time or where the organization seems to be doing well. The white water of this turbulent environment does not allow for complacency any longer. It is critical that the leader remains on the alert and looking proactively rather than reactively at their organization.

Resistance to Change

Resistance to change can be somewhat linked to complacency, but it does not need to be. Leaders are the ones that are going to carry the vision and fulfill the mission of their organizations, and that can only be done by being an effective change agent. If a leader is the one resistant to the changes, the staff will never accept them, and worse, the staff also becomes resistant to change.

Ego Issues

Ego is a very important contribution to who we are as individuals. Everyone has an ego, which is necessary for our personal growth and societal salvation, but the concern is when the ego is out of control to the point that the leader feels that they are the best, the only person with the ability to make decisions and more important than the followers. An inflated ego will alienate followers as well as colleagues in the work environment. Because the ego impacts our behaviors, we will discuss this concept in depth later in the book.

Inability to Communicate a Vision

One of the most important responsibilities of a leader is to be able to communicate a vision and build a compelling case as to why all employees need to align with that vision. When I enter an organization to begin a leadership evaluation, one of the first questions I ask the staff when I round and meet with them is, "What is the vision and mission of the organization?" I am astounded that very often the staff has no idea what the vision and mission of the organization is. It is impossible to lead an organization to success if the staff does not know what that success point is. It is also my experience that when a leader cannot communicate a vision, there are usually also problems with effective communication across the organization.

Ineffective Responses to Challenges

All leaders have varying skills based on their passion and experience. My strengths as a leader reside in strategy and leadership development. Even though I had to be able to manage finances and process improvement, these skills did not excite me in the same way as my passion does. Regardless, the leader needs to be able to meet any challenge no matter how uncomfortable it is for them. One example is the inability of some leaders to approach and deal effectively with conflict. I have always said that what you ignore in the work environment you endorse. Despite how uncomfortable a leader may be with conflict, they need to be able to effectively deal with it. There is usually a host of experts to call upon for support or direction in an organization, and seeking advice is not a sign of weakness, but rather a sign of strength.

Inability to Read the Political Landscape

Political savvy is a critical skill for effective leaders; however, oftentimes some leaders are not able or willing to work within the political framework of an organization. Politics are everywhere, and the political landscape is unique to every organization. Leaders cannot get work done alone. They need the support of their staff, but also the collaboration of colleagues and other individuals in the organization. Leaders that understand the politics of the organization know how to navigate the system and have a better chance of getting their goals achieved and their strategies in place.

Case for the Phoenix Leader

This first chapter was a primer in leadership theory designed to help you begin to analyze your skills and begin thinking of your current level of organizational leadership. It is also a time for you to evaluate your staff and identify their characteristics and what would help inspire them.

The next step is to begin your personal leadership transformation. I have found that the best leaders have been those who are open-minded and can continually reinvent themselves to meet the needs of the changing landscape in their industry and organization. I use the metaphor of a phoenix to describe this strategy. Metaphors are powerful and improve the effectiveness of communication through linkages of unlike concepts. Lumby and English (2010) describe that the use of metaphors has the power to stir imagination and frame agendas. They also identify that people have a tendency to think in pictures, and metaphors help illustrate communication through a pictorial context. Powerful images create powerful messages, and the image of the phoenix is powerful. Metaphors can be a powerful leadership tool if used effectively.

The phoenix is a mythical bird that has the ability to leave its current body and emerge into a new and beautiful being. The phoenix leader is a master of reinvention of self but also inspires his or her teams to think differently and reinvent themselves. Studying the phoenix can provide valuable insights into the acceptance of change, the concepts of resilience and ultimately increased relevance to the organization.

> The metaphor is perhaps one of man's most fruitful potentialities.
> Its efficacy verges on magic.
>
> **Jose Ortegy y Gassett (1925)**

Application to Practice

Following every chapter, there will be a section called "Application to Practice" to help you reflect on the learning of the previous chapter as well as to begin identifying strategies to apply these concepts immediately to your environment. For this chapter, there are four exercises to ponder:

1. Review all the various leadership approaches and identify those that you use in your practice.
2. Evaluate whether you feel that these leadership approaches are effective for you.
3. Evaluate the characteristics of your staff and align them with the appropriate leadership approaches based on your assessment.
4. Reflect on the concept of metaphors and identify your level of utilization of them in your communication strategies.

Chapter 2

The Phoenix Leader

People who soar are those who refuse to sit back and wish things would change.

Charles Swindoll

The metaphor of the phoenix is a powerful image for leaders to aspire to. Because of its powerful imagery, the word *phoenix* is used as both a noun and an adjective. To make the connection between the phoenix and leadership, it is important to first understand the fascinating story of the phoenix.

Story of the Phoenix

Although we have a tendency to think about the phoenix in the context of Greek mythology, the story of the phoenix is a global myth that has roots in many countries. Regardless of the country of origin, the story is the same. The phoenix was also the bird on the first Great Seal of the United States in 1782, until it was replaced by the eagle in the early 1900s.

The phoenix, also called the bird of fire, lays no eggs and has no young or mates. The phoenix is described as majestic and beautiful, with feathers of brilliant colors of red, blue, gold and yellow, somewhat resembling the colors of a peacock. The longevity of the phoenix depends on the belief of the various countries, ranging from 500 to 2400 years. When the phoenix becomes tired, it has the power to ignite into flames, burning itself and leaving behind a pile of silver-grey ashes in the nest. Out of the ashes, the young phoenix emerges and grows to adulthood, once again brilliantly beautiful and strong. The young phoenix then collects the ashes and binds them together with myrrh and delivers an egg to the altar to honor their god (Hamilton, 1998).

Classic Arabian Phoenix

The Arabian phoenix is the most well known throughout history. This image is one of a large bird, as large as an eagle and brilliantly colored with a sweet melodic song that was said to enchant the gods. Recognized attributes of this version of the phoenix include the abilities of reinvention and rebirth. It is also recognized as a figure of high integrity and gentleness that eats only dew, never killing or harming anything around it and preserving all that it touches (Leafloor, n.d.).

The Bennu

The Bennu is the Egyptian description of the phoenix. It is described as a very large bird similar to the great heron, with two large feathers on top of its head. Also, brilliantly colored, this bird is associated with creativity and prosperity, as it was believed to protect the Nile River. It was also associated with the sun, as one of the most vital components of life on earth, and the notion of constancy.

Fenghuang

Fenghuang is the Chinese phoenix. Chinese mythology characterizes this bird as a symbol of majesty, high virtue and grace. It also is believed to have the power to unite the yin and the yang and maintain a sense of harmony. It symbolizes loyalty and honesty with high moral values. The Chinese phoenix is described a bit differently than the others, with a large beak, long snakelike neck and tail of a fish, but also brilliantly colored in hues of red and gold.

Hou-Ou

The Japanese phoenix is called hou-ou. In pictures, this version of the phoenix is similar to that of the Chinese fenghuang. The Japanese characterize this phoenix as representing justice, fidelity and obedience.

Native American Thunderbird

The thunderbird is a powerful cross-cultural element of Native North American mythology. As in the other examples, the thunderbird was a very large, majestic and colorful creature with strong wings that, when beating, could generate thunderstorms and change the weather. As rain provides necessary water to the earth, it is associated with growth and abundance as well as power (Mizrach, 2016).

Characteristics of the Phoenix

Each culture discussed a number of characteristics and attributes of their particular version of the phoenix, all of them positive and many of them applicable to effective leadership. Here is the list.

reinvention	rebirth	integrity	gentleness
creative	prosperity	constancy	high virtue
grace	uniting	loyal	honest
moral	just	fidelity	obedience
power	growth	abundance	resilience

Attributes of the Phoenix Leader

Based on my experience, research and the attributes of the phoenix, I would identify the following as attributes of the phoenix leader. We will study all these later, but they serve as an introduction to how the concept of the phoenix lends itself to leadership.

Strong Sense of Self

In order to understand and lead others, you must first seek to understand yourself. Personal values and behaviors contribute both positively and negatively to leadership scenarios. When you understand yourself, however, you have a better chance of managing yourself effectively to contribute in a positive way to the environment and challenging scenarios.

Effective Interpersonal Relationships

A successful leader needs to be the master of communication and effective interpersonal relationships. This requires a high degree of both emotional and social intelligence and the ability to care about the growth and success of others. This also relates to the ability to effectively manage teams and to be able to reach across all disciplines for consensus and the willingness of others to work together for a common goal. This is a leader that inspires rather than directs, which creates an enjoyable journey for the staff.

Ability to Build an Empowered Workforce

As mentioned in Chapter 1, the leadership approaches that result in the highest degree of staff engagement and productivity are those that are participatory in nature. Transformational leadership has been identified as the most effective approach to leadership with any highly trained professional workers, such as in the healthcare and technology environments. The effective leader needs to be able to build an environment of empowerment that inspires creativity and the ability of the staff to function at their best.

Innovative

Webster (2017) defines *innovation* as simply the act or process of introducing new ideas, devices or methods. Other powerful synonyms associated with the notion of innovation are *change, upheaval, breakthroughs, transformation* and *metamorphosis*. The effective leader needs to be the master of change and reinvention, as the phoenix is.

Resilience

Change implies that one must let go of one thing in exchange for another. What allows for this is the concept of resilience. The phoenix leader is resilient. Ovans (2015) described that not only are leaders with a high degree of resilience more successful in their careers, but also their organizations perform at a higher level than others in their industry. Resilient leaders look at any success, as well as failures, both professional and personal, as positive learning experiences. Resilient people possess three distinct characteristics:

1. An unwavering acceptance of reality
2. A strong set of personal values that life is meaningful
3. An uncanny ability to improvise

In *Psychology Today*, Knaus (2016) describes resilience as a quality whereby people can be "knocked down" by life yet come back stronger than before with a stronger resolve to carry on. They find a way to "rise from the ashes," as the phoenix does. He further describes that some of the factors that make people resilient include a positive attitude, optimism, an ability to know and control their emotions and an understanding of failure as a form of helpful feedback. They simply change course. One of my staff gave me a beautiful plaque that I still keep on my desk today that helps me focus and have hope. That plaque says,

> You will never know the strength of the anchor without the fury of the storm.

Author unknown

Reason for becoming a Phoenix Leader

So, what is the reason to align with a strong metaphor such as the phoenix leader? What are the advantages? I would be naïve to think that everyone is totally altruistic with their career choices. If we were, we would not expect a paycheck. My original reason for becoming a nurse, which was my chosen profession, was to have a great, flexible job while I was pursuing my professional dance career in New York. It was not until I graduated that I realized the passion that grew in me for this calling to nursing. Then I found leadership and focused on growing others and achieving organizational success as I moved up the leadership latter to the C-suite.

The phoenix leader exemplifies excellence in leadership and is an expert in self-reflection, improvement and innovation. This makes this type of leader incredibly valuable to the organization; so here are the four reasons I see for embracing the concepts in this book:

■ Relevance
■ Resilience
■ Personal growth and success
■ Contribution to great work

Relevance

Turnover of senior leadership in all organizations is tremendously high, and much of the turnover is not voluntary. In the past 5 years, CEO transitions have continued to increase, dropping the median tenure rate even more over time.

Marcec (2018), in a recent Equilar study, identified that the new median tenure for CEOs at large-cap (S&P 500) companies was 5.0 years at the end of 2017. This figure continues to drop by a whole year with every analysis. Marcec further describes that the average tenure by long-standing CEOs with several decades of service also dropped in that timeframe.

Batcheller (2010), in her review of the literature on chief nursing officer (CNO) turnover, identified that 40% of CNOs leave their positions within the first year. Twenty-five percent of them were asked to leave. Concurrently, a study of the American College of Healthcare Executives (ACHE) found chief executive officer turnover rates in healthcare organizations to be 18%, although they did not mention how much of that was involuntary versus voluntary separation. Regardless, the reality is that the seats at the top in all industries are continuously vacating, and a good percentage of this is involuntary. So why are these leaders being terminated? Why did they fall out of grace with their leaders? Was it that they became complacent and either unwilling or unable to change? Was it because they lost alignment with the organization and were considered a liability or barriers to change? Without further study, we will never know the answers to these questions. What we do know, however, is that these leaders for some reason became irrelevant to their organization. Adopting the philosophy of continuous renewal and learning, as in the metaphor of the phoenix, can help maintain relevance to the organization, hence improving job security.

Resilience

Webster (2017) defines *resilience* as the ability to come back from a crisis and move forward. The ability to bounce back into shape. Ovans (2015) discussed the work of Richard Farson and Ralph Keyes, who argue that leaders need to become "failure tolerant," by creating a culture whereby one can sidestep resilience by treating both setbacks and successes as positive learning opportunities. Martin Seligman built on this notion, saying that it is also critically important to build resilient employees by breaking down bureaucratic barriers and helping them see the positives in all the scenarios.

Changing the mindset in these situations is powerful because it allows for personal choice as to how to view and react to the issues.

Personal Growth and Success

Every employee stays in their roles for reasons that advantage them, whether it be personal satisfaction, money or a whole host of other personal reasons. Leaders have many personal reasons as well, but two of them are personal growth and success. Adopting the phoenix metaphor as one of continual change and renewal will provide the potential for tremendous personal growth through learning. This knowledge can then be applied to the organization.

Contribution to Great Work

Our work life is a calling, and leadership in any industry is far from easy. It is, however, extremely rewarding when we feel successful in what we are doing. By continual renewal, the phoenix leader finds creative ways to make impactful and more profound contributions to a body of great work.

THE PHOENIX

He knows his time is out! And doth provide
New principles of life; herbs he brings dried
From the hot hills, and with rich spices frames
A Pile shall burn, and Hatch him with his flames.

On this the weakling sits; salutes the Sun
With pleasant noise, and prays and begs for some
Of his own fire, that quickly may restore
The youth and vigor, which he had before.
Whom soon as Phoebus spies, stopping his rays
He makes a stand, and thus allays his pains …
He shakes his locks, and from his golden head,
Shoots on bright beam, which smites with vital fire

The willing bird; to burn is his desire.
That he may live again; he's proud in death,
And goes in haste to gain a better breath.
The spice heap fired with celestial rays
Doth burn the aged Phoenix, when straight stays
The Chariot of the amazed Moon; the pole
Resists the wheeling, swift Orbs, and the whole
Fabric of Nature at a stand remains.
Till the old bird anew, young begins again.

Claudian

Chapter 3

Attributes of the Phoenix Leader, a Strong Sense of Self

Success is liking yourself, liking what you do, and liking how you do it.

Maya Angelou

The phoenix continually reinvents itself when it senses that change is needed. Effective leaders also need to reinvent themselves and their thought processes to meet the demands of the changing environment. You cannot change without the realization that you need to change, which will only manifest if you know yourself. This chapter is about personal understanding of self, what makes us who we are and why is it important.

Values

Values are derived from our belief systems. They shape our desires, behaviors and aspirations that direct what we want to do with our lives. Values are not right or wrong; they are simply a part of who we are. All of us possess particular value systems that are uniquely different from each other, and those values can change over time. The changes are a result of exposure to circumstances or experiences throughout our lives (Spence et al., 2001).

Differences in values can account for the synergy as well as tension that we find in our lives and more globally in our society. Can you imagine what it would be like if we all had the same set values or if we all had the same belief system? It would be incredibly boring. We would have no excitement or diversity in our lives. We would all think alike, desire the same things and function the same way, somewhat like a "Stepford wife" approach to life. Organizations would lack the diversity of creativity and would not be able to progress in new and creative ways, and nothing would get done.

As a society, we share many common values and beliefs. Freedom is a common value that we share in our country, but the intensity of our values and behaviors may vary greatly between individuals. For instance, let us look at the value of achievement. Some people are high achievers while others may not share the same level of drive. Collaboration is another common value that is shared with great variability. Some people like to work with others, and some people like to work alone. You probably can identify people like this in your work setting. Most people value friendship; however, there are those who claim that they do not have friends, nor do they need them. What about humor? I'm sure you have worked with people or have been around people that are funny and enjoyable to be with because they incorporate humor into their lives. Integrity is another strong value that can guide behaviors. There are examples all through the media that identify individuals that lack integrity. Other values may include things like personal development, pleasure and recognition. Religion is a very strong value system in our culture for most people, as is self-respect. These values frame who you are and ultimately guide your behavior.

Where Do Values Come From?

Values can arise from a variety of sources. As children, values can be established by our learning and growth process. Therefore, our early values come from our childhood experiences, with many of them originating from the core values of our parents. I am sure you remember all those old sayings your parents had to keep you in line. "Do your homework," "Clean your room," "Don't talk back," "Say please and thank you," Say you're sorry" and "Don't hit your little brother." All these expressions were driven by a set of core values that your parents subscribed to. They were instilling values to drive your behaviors throughout life (Gokenbach, 2007b).

Both of my parents were schoolteachers. The fact that they believed in the value of education led to this strong value in my siblings and me. Perhaps that is why I continued pursuing advanced degrees and have committed myself to a journey of lifelong learning. In other words, my parents' value of education molded my behavior and probably much of my success. They were also very religious, so faith and religion became core values during those early years and have remained with me into adulthood.

Values also come from our personal experiences. If you have had a brush with death or are facing the challenges of a serious disease, you may have a different appreciation for life or a little more respect for your health than someone who has not had that experience.

I have been a director of critical care and emergency services for many years. I could always identify values in our nurses by observing them caring for patients. They all seemed to have a deeper sense of empathy and compassion in dealing with death and dying if they had a personal experience with death or loss in their own families. They could empathize with the people that were experiencing a personal tragedy. I also observed that nurses who were parents related more intimately with the parents of children that had died or were seriously ill. That is not to say that all our nurses were not superb and effective in their communication with patients, all of them do a wonderful job. In my experience, however, there seems to be a deeper understanding of pain and sorrow, which translates to the communication patterns with the patients and families when those experiences were realized.

Alignment of Values and Behaviors

Values need to be aligned with our behaviors in order for us to feel good about ourselves and be successful. There are several leadership publications that address the concept of value alignment as a critical success factor in all we do in our jobs, careers and personal goals.

Here is another profound example to ponder. I have had the opportunity to merge five hospitals over my career in healthcare administration. Earlier in my nursing administration experience, I was responsible for merging two extremely different hospitals into one hopefully big happy family. Mergers and acquisitions are always very stressful for the staff affected and never are a welcomed experience. Even healthy mergers that eventually lead to strong organizations begin with fear and turmoil. Cultural issues and a lack of quality leadership may lead some of these organizations to fail.

In my personal experience, in relation to our discussion of values, one of these hospitals was Catholic and run by the Sisters of Mercy, and the other was not. The hospital that I worked in was the non-Catholic hospital and also the purchasing organization. Although we had many examples of culture clashes throughout the organization, there was one very profound misalignment of values. This was difficult to overcome in the context of this merger, resulting in the loss of nursing staff. My organization performed medically indicated abortions in the obstetrical department, which were prohibited by the faith-based organization. This created incredible conflict with many of the nurses in the faith-based organization since they were now expected to practice outside their belief system. Although we did not expect them to alter their values and perform the abortions, many of them could not accept the fact that the hospital was going to continue to perform them. This resulted in many nurses struggling with a choice that did not feel good to them, causing a significant percentage of them to seek employment elsewhere.

The above example is profound in that religious values were involved. Mergers and acquisitions in any organization regardless of the industry disrupts culture and strains the value system of the organizations affected.

Regardless of the circumstance, it is vital that you remain true to your values and that those values are aligned with behaviors and choices you make in your life, whether that be in your job, family or personal situations. This also demonstrates the strength of commitment to your personal values. At times, we find ourselves in situations that create conflict and cause us to struggle with personal dilemmas. Perhaps you work with a boss that you do not agree with regard to work ethic or practice. Maybe you have a friend or colleague that is in conflict with your value system. These situations can cause tension in your life since they are not aligned with your personal values, and therefore don't feel "right" to you.

Finding Your Personal Values: An Exercise

Every leader who knows themselves should be able to immediately list their top five personal values. From an application to leadership perspective, they may dictate your behaviors in certain scenarios. The following is a quick and easy exercise to identify your values.

Directions:

Quickly read through the list of common core values; do not think about it. List the five values that you think most represent yourself (there will be many of them; we are only looking for the top five). Once you have identified your values, number them from 1 to 5, with number 1 being your most important.

Once you identify your personal values, you can use these as a template for your choices and align your life. My core values in order from most important to least are family, spirituality, health and wellness, integrity and lifelong learning. An example of alignment for me is the fact that since learning is so important to me, as long as I am engaging in learning, I am fulfilled. Whether that is learning in the work setting, coaching others, teaching or taking a class unrelated to my work, that aligns with my core value for lifelong learning. Also, I feel the best when I am with my family, especially since that is my number one core value (Figure 3.1).

VALUES ANALYSIS EXERCISE

Values analysis:	Check
Achievement (attaining goals, feeling of accomplishment)	_____
Advancement (growth of department and each other)	_____
Adventure (willing to take risks, try new processes)	_____
Competition (strive to be the best)	_____
Collaboration (work well with others)	_____
Economic Stability (balance budget, cost conscious)	_____
Education (school, learning)	_____
Empowerment (able to contribute and make relevant decisions)	_____
Fairness (treat everyone the same, review all situations)	_____
Family (focus on any family members)	_____
Friendship (close relationship with each other)	_____
Health (self care, health habits, exercise, nutrition)	_____
Helpfulness (willing to assist each other)	_____
Humor (believe in the power of laughter)	_____
Inclusion (desires to be included with others)	_____
Integrity (high level of honesty, true to beliefs)	_____
Involvement (active participation with others)	_____
Loyalty (committed to department and role)	_____
Order (believe in the need for organization and structure)	_____
Perseverance (strength despite challenges)	_____
Personal Development (help each other to improve and grow)	_____
Pleasure (strive to make the job fun)	_____
Power (influence, importance, authority)	_____
Recognition (receive and give acknowledgment)	_____
Religion (strong belief in faith)	_____
Relationships (belief in the need for relationships)	_____
Responsibility (accountable, reliable)	_____
Self-Respect (self-esteem, believe in the team)	_____
Spirituality (possess a belief in faith)	_____
Teamwork (work together, support all team members)	_____
Wealth (desire more resources)	_____
Wisdom (support knowledge and education)	_____

Figure 3.1 Values analysis exercise.

Values-Based Leadership

Haden and Jenkins (2015) describe values as vital to leadership but also discuss the importance of virtue, which they relate to as excellence in character that is shaped by actions into habitual ways of thinking. They purport that virtue applies to life and therefore is the heart of effective leadership in thriving organizations. The nine virtues that they have identified as important are humility, honesty, courage, perseverance, hope, charity, balance, wisdom and justice.

They also support the notion of moral goodness as important and align that with the notion of ethics, which is what constitutes morality and moral behavior. Their nine virtues fit nicely into this framework. I see that these virtues flow from our values as subtitles that further direct behavior.

Tom and Susan Kuczmarski (1995) in their book *Values-Based Leadership* speak to the importance of consistency between the leaders' core value and the organization. Strong, consistent values can help align the organization and engage the staff in the mission and vision moving toward a common goal. The best leaders exhibit both their personal values and their ethical beliefs in their leadership style, which engenders trust in the staff (Heathfield, 2016). This consistent practice of demonstrating values and virtues is authentic and sends a powerful message that can help to engender trust. Authenticity is now being discussed as a necessary practice for leaders to successfully lead their organizations.

Authenticity Defined

To thine own self be true.

Polonius, *Hamlet*

"Authenticity is the degree to which you are true to your personality, spirit and character" (Hollis, 2008: 2). It is based in self-knowledge and connecting with your inner voice, who you are as a person. Being authentic requires that you reinvent yourself by overcoming the past and moving to a new beginning of truly being who you are. Norma Hollis is one of America's leading authenticity experts and has published many books on this topic. She has identified 10 steps to achieving authenticity of self, which then can be applied to other scenarios, such as leadership. Here are her 10 steps, which I will define in the context of healthcare leadership.

Hollis's 10 Steps to Authenticity

1. *Intuition*: We all have an inner voice that speaks to us all the time, whether we are conscious of it or not. Oftentimes, we are so busy and distracted that we don't listen to it. This is your intuition. Based on your values and experiences, you inherently know what you need to know. I am sure you have had experiences where you wanted to do one thing but your inner voice told you something different, which unnerved you and may have changed your mind. I have always told my kids, "When in doubt, don't." I see leadership as both and art and a science. Theory and research is the science and intuition is the art. Listen to it. The best decisions apply several methods of analysis, review of data and analytics, review of literature or other evidence and intuition. Once all the analysis is done, does it feel good? The answer to that will be your intuition. I have had many experiences where the feeling was just not right, so I did not move forward with the decision. That decision to not move forward was always the right one that left me with no regrets.

2. *Live by your values*: We spoke a great deal about values in the previous section. Authenticity is the process of being true to those values and never wavering from them. Compromising your core values is inauthentic and can result in personal conflict. In a leadership position, your savvy staff will know if you are inauthentic and will not trust you.

3. *Inspiration*: Moving forward with any initiative and achieving any goal requires inspiration. Oftentimes, we look to the outside for this inspiration when the real inspiration needs to come from within. Motivational speakers, books and programs are valuable to our growth. We think they inspire us, but what they do is provide the information and ideas to become inspired. If you are inspired and you share that excitement, you have a better chance of your staff being inspired.

4. *Be well*: In my mind, leadership is an athletic endeavor. It is challenging both physically and emotionally, which requires a healthy, strong body. I do not know of any executive that works less than 50 hours a week and some much more. You cannot run this type of marathon without stamina. Authenticity is caring for all components of the human being in a holistic way. We will discuss this later, but living a healthy life will give you the energy you need to effectively lead.

5. *Surround yourself with authentic people*: All of us serve a variety of roles in our lives; we may be parents, leaders, friends and, some of us,

many more. These are both personal and professional networks that we reside in. Unfortunately, for the most part, your professional network based on your career and job is chosen for you when you decide to accept a position. In my executive experience, I have encountered many individuals that were far from authentic. Identify those in your work network that are authentic and align with them. Externally you have the ability to select your network of friends and acquaintances. Choose those that are authentic who can also help support you in your quest for authenticity.

6. *Think abundance*: When we think of abundance, we have a tendency to think about money and "stuff" when the term means so much more. Being authentic requires an expanded concept of wealth that includes valuable intangibles and the ability to be grateful for what we have. I believe that every day is a gift and an opportunity to serve. We are never guaranteed tomorrow, only the present, which I believe is truly a gift. That is why it is called a present. The authentic person has this expanded concept of wealth that is far more than monetary.

7. *Honor and share your gifts*: All human beings are born with their own unique set of both intellectual and spiritual gifts. Once you recognize what your gifts are, you can capitalize on them, cultivate them and share them with others. Leadership gives you an amazing opportunity to share those gifts with those around you through mentoring, coaching, supporting and growing others to be the best they can be. Leadership is not about you but rather your contribution to the greater good.

8. *Enhance your personality*: Your personality is the first thing that people see and react to either positively or negatively. Whether you realize it or not, this becomes your personal brand. We are judged on first impressions, which leave a lasting perception on those who we interact with. To be an effective leader, that impression needs to be positive. An authentic person understands that personality comprises emotions, thoughts and behavioral patterns, and they have the capacity to learn how to always display their best. There are times we all become frustrated and angry, but if we are authentic, we continue to realize the potential effects of these emotions on others and work to keep them positive.

9. *Tweak your lifestyle*: Part of knowing yourself is to understand your daily patterns and habits, which all tie into your lifestyle. We all have limited energy, and how we use that energy can contribute to our level

of authenticity. It is also impossible to promote something that you do not personally model. If you encourage your staff to be physically fit and you are not, that is not authentic. If you want moral staff, you need to display your morality and be consistent in that modeling.

10. *Align yourself:* Lastly, alignment simply means to reflect on the elements we discussed and work to maintain the behaviors and thoughts necessary to keep you authentic.

Authentic Leadership

Once you align your authentic life, you can adapt it to your leadership. Kuczmarski and Kuczmarski (1995) defined *authentic leadership* as being you when you are supposed to be you. They further described that if you simply "adopt" a leadership style to fit into, that in and of itself is not authentic. An authentic leader develops their own unique style and remains consistent in their behaviors. George (2003) stated that effective leadership begins with authenticity. He identified several qualities of the authentic leader, which include

- Has an interest in empowering others
- Is guided by compassion and heart
- Draws on the inspiration from themselves to help inspire others
- Is the master of reinvention and able to adapt to any situation
- Is not afraid to make mistakes and admit those mistakes

Kruse (2013) identified several other qualities of the authentic leader:

- Has a high level of self-awareness
- Is mission driven and focused on results
- Has the confidence to focus on the long term

Using the metaphor of the phoenix, it is clear to see that the attributes of the authentic leader align very well. If we do not live our lives as who we are, we will be in eternal conflict. I have witnessed chief executive officers (CEOs) and leaders that truly believed that they could not be real in the work environment for fear of being perceived as soft or weak. Their ego would not let them be perceived as anything but powerful. The opposite is true. Power comes from being an authentic person.

All about Ego

Have you ever met an individual with an ego the size of the northern hemisphere? Of course, you have! I can name hundreds of them that I have met in my lifetime, and it was not uncommon that this ego ultimately got in the way of their success. The good news is that ego is an important element of who we are and important for self-confidence and self-promotion. It then makes sense to say that most leaders have big egos. The problem is not the ego in and of itself; it is controlling the ego through preventing behaviors that can be damaging in both the work and private environments. So, let us investigate the theories behind the ego.

Ego Defined

Sigmund Freud (2012) was the most preeminent theorist about the science of the mind. He developed the psychoanalytic theory of personality development founded on the basis of conflict between different segments of the mind, the id, ego and superego. Although Freud has been criticized about the fact that much of his theory was based on sexual development, he also did not carry out clinical empirical studies to substantiate his theories; regardless, his theories continue to be incorporated into modern psychology today. Investigating the three levels of personality does shed some light on the source of behaviors.

Superego

As we grow and develop as children, we are molded by our environment to adopt a series of values, behaviors and beliefs that help us fit into our culture. The superego is considered the highest level of moral personality and does not waver from what subconsciously the mind thinks is right. The superego keeps us aligned with what is perceived acceptable behavior in society.

Id

In direct opposition to the superego is the id. This part of the mind is the most primitive and is only interested in what it wants and what will satisfy basic physical needs and urges. In our civilized culture, it is impossible to allow the id to control behavior. For instance, if you have something I want, the id would direct me to take it with no remorse. I just want it. The id and the superego need a moderator to merge both desires and moral conscience, and that is the ego.

Ego

Henriques (2013) defines the ego as the extent to which one thinks highly of one's self. It is responsible for the regulation of behavior in compliance with culture to help the individual fit into society. Cherry (2016c) described that the ego is the component of personality that prevents us from acting on our basic urges and functions on both a subconscious and conscious level (Figure 3.2). As infants in the world, we are perfect little creatures with no psychological issues involving the ego since it has not been developed. The ego evolves over time with our personal development experiences that mold us into who we are.

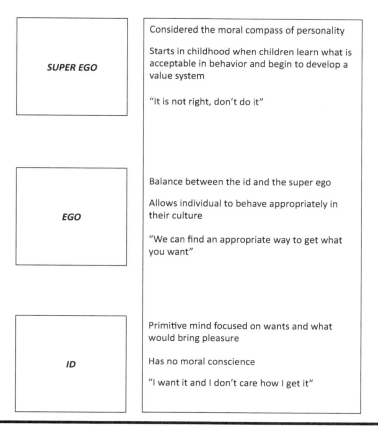

Figure 3.2 Components of the mind.

Ego as the Enemy

So, what does this mean for leadership? The inability to control the ego is the enemy of effective leadership and ultimately success throughout life. Holiday (2016) described the external versus internal loci of control in relation to ego. Those individuals that find it difficult to control the ego view the world as external to them; in other words, failures are a product of the outside world and what it does to them. They are extrinsic thinkers. Conversely, those who have control of their ego realize that ego is a potential enemy that lies within. These individuals have an internal locus of control and a perception that they have more control of their choices and destiny. In the case of perceived failure, the intrinsic thinker will initially look to themselves to evaluate what they could have done better to change the outcome. An inflated ego can impede learning and stifle growth of talent. It can blind us to our faults and make recovery from failure difficult to impossible (Holiday, 2016).

Common Ego Traps to Avoid

Harvard Business Review published a study that suggested that two in five CEOs fail within 18 months of leading their organization secondary to the inability to identify and control their ego. Shirkani (2013) identified eight ego traps that will destroy a leader's career:

1. *Ignoring feedback you don't like*: If you feel that you are the best of the best, you are not going to believe that any feedback that you don't like is reality. Effective leaders are first of all not afraid of feedback and, especially with negative feedback, take the opportunity to learn from it. Negative feedback probably does not feel good to most people, but it is the way you look at the opportunities that will help you actually strengthen your leadership skills if addressed.
2. *Believing your technical skills are enough*: Once you believe that you have nothing more to learn, you stifle your opportunity to learn. Shirkani describes that these types of leaders lose flexibility, self-control and social skills. They revel in people telling them that they are a genius. If we look back to the phoenix, reinvention and rebirth are totally contrary to this type of leader. Effective leaders realize that every opportunity is an opportunity to learn.

3. *Only surrounding yourself with people like you*: If you put people around you that are like-minded, you do not have to listen to conflicting viewpoints that may prove that you are not as great as you think you are. Great leaders put a collection of individuals around them that have a variety of skillsets despite the discomfort of working with them. The only way to prevent group-think and make better informed decisions is to have robust discussions that represent varying viewpoints and enhance the learning of the group. Group-think is a phenomenon that happens in scenarios where the leader is excessively strong or the group is not diverse. Decisions are myopic in character and can lead to disastrous circumstances and substandard decisions.

4. *Not letting go of control*: Leaders cannot do it all, even though some of them think they can. Oppressive control over your staff will stifle creativity, kill the concept of empowerment and decrease staff engagement. It is virtually impossible to build a team when you feel you are the only important entity on that team that has the knowledge and ability to get the work done. Growing others and letting them do their jobs increases trust, staff satisfaction and ultimately productivity.

5. *Being blind to your downstream impact*: It is critical that leaders need to be aware of their actions and what can happen based on their decisions. Outcomes of all decisions are not always what we expect, but when things go wrong, it is an opportunity to learn from what happened and correct it. If a leader does not have that level of insight, when problems arise secondary to decisions, they cannot see that it is a result of something that they did. They will look for external excuses to explain away the problem as not their fault. Even worse, they sacrifice their subordinates as scapegoats, throwing them to the wolves. I have also watched high-ego leaders refuse to recognize failure of their own decisions to the point that they allowed for money to be lost for the organization rather than them look unsuccessful. Many have been relieved of their roles secondary to this blind spot.

6. *Underestimating how much you are being watched*: Your staff and other people in the organization are always watching you and everything you do (Shirkani, 2013). I will expand on this concept a bit to introduce the concept of a personal brand. We all have them whether we realize it or not. If you think of a brand, it is really being more of the

experience that people have when they encounter you. The brand can be positive or negative. If you are the type of leader that creates your own set of rules that are different from those around you, you will have set yourself above them and they will sense that you believe you are better than them. You are a continual role model, whether you realize it or not.

7. *Losing touch with the frontline experience*: I will say this a hundred times in this book—the farther you are away from the front line, the less right you have to make decisions that affect those on the front line. I always felt that I was an accomplished clinical nurse, which is why I received my first leadership promotion early in my career. As I began to move up the corporate ladder, I became less of a clinician and more of an executive. Especially in healthcare, where the environment is constantly changing, executives need a reality check as to what is really happening at the point of service. I am going to cover this in depth when we get to the topic of visibility, but it is important to set the context for the discussion later on.

8. *Relapsing back to your old ways*: The phoenix reinvents itself as all leaders need to do. The problem is that as you work on improving your leadership persona and skills, you cannot allow yourself to revert to the old ways of doing things when you are not happy with the outcomes. I always talk about the concept of "baby steps" as we continue on our quest to self-improvement, and as human beings we will make mistakes along the way. We just need to be cognizant of our behaviors at all times and quickly correct our course when necessary.

Application to Practice

We covered several important concepts to ponder regarding how we apply this to our work environment. Here are some recommendations:

Values analysis: Conduct your values analysis and align your values with your professional and personal lives. Do they fit? You can also present these concepts to your leadership team and conduct that same exercise with them to enhance their insights into themselves.

Authenticity: Think about the concept of authenticity and align your behaviors with Norma Hollis's 10 steps. How authentic are you? What can you do to enhance your level of authenticity? Also, is your leadership team authentic? You can share these concepts with them.

Ego: Reflect on the power of your ego. Is it in control? Review the eight ego traps and see if you are falling into any of them. Also reflect on the levels of ego of your leadership team and see if there is some coaching that can be done about this topic when appropriate.

Chapter 4

Attributes of the Phoenix Leader: Effective Interpersonal Relationships

The function of leadership is to produce more leaders, not more followers.

Ralph Nader

A leader can accomplish absolutely nothing without the trust and support of their staff, and the only way to build that trust is to cultivate effective interpersonal relationships. Trust is extremely difficult to build but extremely easy to lose. Once that bond is broken, it is an uphill battle to rebuild it, if at all possible. The staff needs to believe that you have their best interests at heart. Getting to their hearts, however, requires going through their brains by tapping into the science of emotion. This chapter focuses on several important concepts through a scientific lens, including emotional intelligence (EI) and social intelligence (SI) and the art of communication.

Emotional Intelligence Defined

Daniel Goleman (2006a) defined *emotional intelligence* as the ability to recognize, understand and manage our own emotions but also to recognize, understand and influence the emotions of others. I define it a bit more simply. There are three sides to every story, yours, mine and what really

happened, and I respect and honor your point of view and recognize that I see things differently. In yoga, the term *namaste* means the light in me recognizes and honors the light in you. We all see things through our own set of lenses, and that is not right or wrong; it is just the way we see the situation based on our experiences and our value system. Conversely, the other side is not wrong either; it is simply their way of seeing things from their experiences and value systems.

The Story of Nikki

As my kids were growing up, I prided myself on making all their Halloween costumes, from the first little bunny outfit on their first Halloween through the years to the last time they wanted to dress up. When my daughter was 16, I was doing a great deal of traveling, so I told her if she wanted me to make her a costume, she needed to let me know as soon as possible so I could get the materials and make it before my next upcoming trip. Of course, as a teenager other things seemed to get in the way, so she did not really think about what she wanted to be until the last minute. I was very stressed with the upcoming travel and frustrated that I could not get a costume done for her in time. My husband said he would handle it and take her shopping to get her something to wear. This would free me up to concentrate on my work. My husband is always very helpful and supportive, so I told him that would be great. While I was away, I called him to check on the progress of her costume and he said that they had it all taken care of and she was going to be an angel. Aw, an angel. In my mind, I saw the costume my mom made for me as a kid. She used a white bed sheet with tinsel stapled to it and cardboard wings—such a sweet image. So I asked him what he bought for her and he went down the list: sequined halter top, large feather wings, rhinestone halo and white fishnet stocking, but they were having a hard time finding white spankies— I was now concerned.

On Halloween, she was going to go to a party with her friends, so while she was getting dressed I poured my wonderful husband a glass of wine and had him sit in the living room next to the open staircase. I wanted him to be the first to see the fruits of his labor as Nikki descended the stairs in all her beauty in her "angel" costume. She was breathtaking in her fishnets, spiked heels, big hair, halter top and wings—a Victoria's Secret Angel. He was astounded and helped her "modify" the outfit a bit, which she was not happy with, but I just smiled and said, "Good job, Dad" (Figure 4.1).

Figure 4.1   Nikki.

I tell this story because it illustrates three different lenses through which to see things. I saw a sweet little girl in a sheet and tinsel, she saw a sexy Victoria's Secret Angel and I have no clue what my husband was thinking. Those interpretations are not wrong, they are just different.

Max DePree (1992) supported the notion of the importance of emotions when he made the comment that "leadership is a serious meddling in the lives of others." Leaders can make or break others, and many leaders do not even realize the effect that they have on the emotions of others, or if they do, they may not care. If I was your boss and I called you at 5:00 p.m. on Friday afternoon and said that I needed to see you in my office first thing on Monday, emotions such as fear and anxiety would take over and probably ruin your weekend and make it difficult for you to look forward to coming to work the following Monday. Now if I called you at 5:00 p.m. on Friday and asked if you could find time in your schedule to see me on Monday to go over the progress of some projects, no big deal, and have a great weekend, you would feel very different about that conversation. We as leaders have that power to make or break those that we work with. That is a power that we cannot abuse.

Emotional Intelligence, the Science

To understand the science behind EI, we must first look at the physiology of the brain. The three areas related to EI are the brainstem, the limbic system and the neocortex. These three areas of the brain work together to provide the foundation for our thought processes and interpretation of data from the outside world, as well as the crafting of our reactions to stimuli (Goleman, 2013; Sterrett, 2014). I truly believe that we as leaders need to get back to the basics of science to understand what we need to do to inspire and lead people. Then we can understand how to craft our strategy to move forward.

First Brain

The brainstem is considered the first brain and is responsible for all of our autonomic responses. Breathing, nerve responses and automatic habits are included in the list of responsibilities for the first brain. Habits are represented here because the brain learns through repetition until it becomes automatic. You do not need to think about how to drive your car since you have trained your brain through repetition. Reflexes that happen automatically are also part of this brain. If you touch something hot, you draw away from it without thinking due to these reflexes. The first brain is a vital component of life.

Emotional Brain

The limbic system is known as the emotional brain and is closely linked to EI. It is related to our emotional experiences through life that build the foundation for intuition, gut feelings and ideas. The more experiences through life, the richer the emotional warehouse is and the more reliable these feelings become. We mentioned these in prior discussion utilizing the term *intuition*. Leadership is both an art and a science. We look at data, analyze information, develop strategies and look at things very objectively. There is, however, a great deal of emotional information to add to the decisions to make even better choices when we tap into our intuition. It is not uncommon for us as adults to ignore this subliminal information in favor of objective data. We have all had situations in our lives where the decisions did not feel right. I have always been of the philosophy that if something does not feel right, do not do it. Work the problem until it feels acceptable on all levels.

Rational Brain

The neocortex is the third brain level, which is also known as the rational brain. This area of the brain helps us with functions that are related to our thinking and thought processes. These include language, planning, strategy, problem solving, critical thinking, decision-making and innovation. This part of the brain is connected to the limbic system through millions of neurons that allow for emotional influences to cross into our thoughts to influence the decisions we ultimately make. This enables the limbic system to make course corrections before the cortex even realizes the issue (Semerda, 2016).

Value to Leadership

Two concepts come into play here, the emotions and ego. It is important to understand the connections between the two and the way these connections lead to behavior. Our discussion on the ego highlighted the fact that the ego is a reflection of how highly one thinks about themselves. The way we feel about ourselves is all about emotions and the limbic system. Literature supports the notion that employees that feel good about themselves are more engaged and productive in their work. The leader then needs to tap into those emotions in a positive way. Elizabeth Jeffries (1992) articulates this beautifully in her book *The Heart of Leadership*, where she highlights the importance of "soft skills" as more important than analytical skills. These soft skills tug at our emotional base and prop up our egos when used in a positive way. When we feel good about ourselves, those feelings translate into everything we do in life, from career to personal scenarios.

Emotional Intelligence and the Phoenix Leader

Just as the phoenix is aware of when it needs to reinvent itself, the phoenix leader is aware of their level of EI and works to develop this skill to its full potential. Throughout my career, I have experienced leaders that have made me feel great about myself as well as those that used their power to devastate everyone around them. I am sure you have as well. It has been helpful for me to observe and reflect on both of those opposing experiences and learn from them by focusing on the behaviors of both types of leaders. As a consultant, when conducting a review of problem areas in an organization, consistently, the areas with high turnover, low morale and decreased productivity have leaders that fail to connect to the hearts of those they lead.

Social Intelligence Defined

EI relates to the ability to connect to a single person with their own individual, personal psychology. This ability to connect to others affects brain chemistry in those we interact with. Leading groups of people in the greater context requires the leader to multiply those effects on many to connect to the brain's social circuitry. There is a great deal of neuroscience research that reveals that our brains are foundationally social, requiring intimate brain-to-brain linkages (Goleman, 2008). These linkages are strongest between individuals that we spend the most time with, and for most of us, that is in the work environment.

Social Intelligence, the Science

As with EI, the brain levels apply; however, with the social brain two new neurons come into play, the spindle cell and the mirror neuron. The spindle cells are the most rapid of any neurons, and they are the ones that guide quick decisions in a social atmosphere and ultimately guide behavior. There are more spindle cells in the human brain than in any other species (Goleman and Boyatzis, 2008). We have all been in uncomfortable social situations from time to time, and the way we react to those scenarios is based on the response of the spindle neurons. You may be sitting in a meeting and a colleague of yours challenges your statement or idea in a negative way. You may have a negative emotional reaction to that, but you rapidly scope the situation and choose to either not react to it or handle the response in a professional way. Individuals with low levels of SI may respond defensively or violently to the same situation.

Mirror neurons are very interesting. They were found by accident by an Italian neuroscientist, Dr. Giacomo Rizzolati, in the 1980s in his research on the brains of monkeys. He found that this particular neuron fired when the monkey was mimicking the movements of the lab assistants. He hypothesized that we fit into our social world either consciously or unconsciously by reading the emotions of others through their behaviors and then reproducing those emotions in ourselves (Winerman, 2005). If a friend of yours has a death in the family, you immediately read their emotions and adjust yours to empathize with them, responding in a comforting way. This is an extremely powerful advantage for leaders in organizations. Goleman (2008) suggested that leaders' emotions and actions will reflect on the followers, who will mirror those feelings and behaviors. This also builds a strong case for leading by example. If you are positive, your staff will be positive; if you are negative, your staff will be negative.

One of my most enjoyable positions as a leader was when I was the manager of an intensive care unit in Detroit, Michigan. I had the greatest staff! Amazing, empowered people. I never had to worry about anything. They did their own schedule (which was unheard of back then), and if someone called in, they would get on the phone and get the vacancy covered. They supported each other, made changes in their work environment to improve efficiencies and the list goes on. My staff satisfaction scores were through the roof and my patient satisfactions scores were that good as well. We had fantastic relationships with our physicians and also had superior quality scores. We all cared for each other and supported each other. When I relocated to Texas, my wonderful staff from 35 years ago actually took me out to dinner before I left. That was such a gift. They gave me a cup that says, "World's best boss" and a necklace that has a family tree image to represent our "family." They are special people.

When I was in this position, every year at Christmas, my husband and I would host a party for the entire staff and everyone who was not working would show up and we partied until the wee hours of the morning. We also sent food to the unit for those who could not attend the party. What was interesting one year was that my husband took a group picture of the staff at the party. Back then, I used to perm my hair so that it was easy to care for

Table 4.1 Emotional versus Social Intelligence

Emotional Intelligence	Social Intelligence
Self-awareness	Social awareness Primal empathy Empathetic accuracy Listening Social cognition
Self-management	Relationship management Synchrony Self-presentation Influence Concern

with my busy schedule. When we looked at the pictures, he noticed something that I did not. Most of the women had the same hairstyle. You could say that it was just the style back then, but I was the first one to adopt it and everyone seemed to follow suit.

If you are aware of it, you can observe mirroring behavior everywhere in the workplace. One team that I worked with over the course of my career had what we called the "head bobbers." Whenever our boss said something, these five ladies would begin nodding their heads. It would start with one and soon they were all doing it, mirroring each other. When one would speed up, they all would speed up. It fascinated me. I was not a head bobber. In your next one-on-one meeting with someone, notice what happens when you scratch your nose, frown or change positions. Chances are that the person you are meeting with is mirroring the same movements all with the unconscious need to socially fit into the situation and link to your brain. Goleman (2006b) summarizes SI abilities in reference to EI (Table 4.1).

Value to Leadership

Ronald Riggio (2014) believes that EI is what we are born with but SI develops over time from our social experiences. Through my experience, I have a tendency to believe that both qualities can be developed through coaching and experience. The following are key elements that he believes can be developed:

1. *Verbal fluency and conversational skills*: This may be more difficult for introverts versus extroverts; however, it can be learned. I have a great friend and mentor and have been blessed to be able to work with her on

many projects. She is very much an introvert. She is a social wizard in the way she engages people and "works the room." At the end of a long "social" day, I would ask her if she wanted to go to dinner and relax for a while, and she would very often say, "No thanks, I need room service and some downtime. Being an introvert, this environment drains my energy." I always honored that in her, especially since she was always tuned into what she personally needed and willingly expressed those needs.

2. *Knowledge of social roles, rules and scripts*: We all play different roles in the different facets of our lives. We may be spouses, parents and employees and be engaged in clubs or organizations. In order for us to effectively socially fit into those various scenarios, we need to know the rules and follow the appropriate scripts. You behave differently with your kids or your friends than you do with your boss. Social roles and rules in an organization are the fabric of its culture. If those roles align with your moral value system, it is critical to conform to them for your success in the organization.

3. *Effective listening skills*: SI is all about the brain-to-brain connection with another person, and the only way to appropriately respond to them is by listening to them. Effective leaders are great listeners who make you feel that you are the only person in the world when you are together. You feel that you provide value to the conversation. I had one of my CEOs that would be in a one-on-one meeting with me and his cell phone would go off. He would simply answer the phone and then get up and walk out of the room to finish his conversation no matter how long it took. If the phone rang in my midsentence—so what? I would sit there and wait for him to return to try to piece back the conversation where we left off. He would do this in large meetings that he would lead as well. His phone would ring and he would get up and leave the room to answer it while all of us would just look at each other and wait until he came back. We all felt that his behavior was incredibly rude and that our time was never as important as his time. We are going to cover this a bit more when we talk about communication, but for now, during meetings have your phone off; tell your administrative assistant to hold all calls and do not be distracted with things on your desk. Make the person in front of you feel that they are the only person in the world for that short period of time.

4. *Understanding what makes other people tick*: This is best accomplished by observation and knowing your audience. I do a great deal of public speaking, presenting across the country, and the first question I ask when invited to speak is to find out who will be in the audience so that I can understand them and find ways to resonate with them. I was

asked to do a presentation on health and wellness for the Michigan Farm Women's Association. Of course, I was talking on health and wellness, one of my specialties, but I needed to know how I could make the topic relate to them and to be real and meaningful for them. I began by researching the organization and issues that were pertinent to them. I began the talk by telling them that my only experience with farming was with the Facebook game Farmville, but I was excited that I bought my first combine machine, which made the harvesting of my crops much easier. Roar of laughter from the crowd; we were connected at that point and they were very receptive to my information.

Think about this in the context of your staff. What are their values, likes or dislikes, and how can you tap into their emotions? When I was running emergency rooms (ERs), we used to laugh that the staff loved to eat, and in the ER, there were many times when we did not get a chance to break for lunch. For meetings and events, I would always make sure that there was food available for them since I knew they appreciated it. I would also order pizza or some other food when I knew that they were so busy that no one was going to get lunch. I have noticed through the management of many different departments that they all had unique cultures, likes and dislikes to tap into. Whenever I got the staff together to meet with me, I provided some type of food for them, whether it was fruit, cookies or muffins, to send a strong message that I cared about them while fulfilling one of their points of enjoyment.

5. *Role-playing and social self-efficacy*: Albert Bandura in 1977 published his seminal work on the concept of self-efficacy as a critical determinant of behavior. He proposed that self-efficacy is the individual's belief in their ability to succeed in a particular situation. In this context, it is the degree of self-confidence that we have that has been built over time through our learning experiences. In leadership, it is the ability to perform confidently in any situation.

As I was promoted from level to level, I was assigned departments that were outside the realm of nursing and clearly outside of my experience base. This was very challenging for me since nursing was my comfort zone; however, I studied, learned, observed and sought the help of experts to gain the background to effectively lead the new departments. I needed to approach these new teams with the confidence that I could help them, especially since many of the physicians had a tendency to compartmentalize nurses as clinical and not as administrators. Despite the initial fear of the unknown, I found the challenge to be very uplifting and energizing. I built a radiology department and Gamma Knife suite, bought countless pieces of technology, built many buildings and so much more, which prepared me for where I am today. One of my mentors told me that you should always apply for a role that you have no idea how to fulfill. This stretches you and forces you to think differently.

I read a study that illustrated the difference between men and women in respect to their perception of ability to perform a role. It was found that men felt comfortable with a new role when they were competent with 15% of the expectations. Conversely, women did not feel confident to pursue a new role until they felt accomplished in 90% of the competencies needed. Women wait too long to take risks or to search for more experiential opportunities to grow their repertoire of skills.

6. *Impression management skills*: First impressions are lasting, and impressions that reoccur time and time again begin to create your personal brand. I mentioned before that the definition of *brand* is the experience that others have when they are with you, as well as what they hear about you through others. Think about sitting outside on a very hot day. You are thirsty. You go to the fridge and get a Coke and a glass of ice. As you pour the drink over the ice, you see the rich color, you hear and see the bubbles, you feel the coolness of the glass, and as you take your first sip, you now taste the great flavor and feel the coolness down your throat as you swallow. Thirst is quenched. You remember the experience of the feelings. If you are socially intelligent, you leave your staff with positive experiences when they encounter you and you build a strong brand for others you encounter around you.

Social Intelligence and the Phoenix Leader

When you think of the majesty of the phoenix, you can readily see a brand of power and beauty. You also notice a high degree of self-confidence in the ability to lead. Effective leadership is not only the ability to effectively reach one heart; you need to collectively reach all hearts, for it is in that greater number that great things will be accomplished.

Strong Communication Skills

Mike Myatt (2012) said that "you cannot be a great leader without being a great communicator however the skills for effective communication are not taught in any academic setting." With this segment, I not only provide you with information about effective communication but also suggest some strategies to build an effective infrastructure for communication in your organization. You cannot effectively manage any process without fully understanding it. In my experience, communication in organizations is a great illusion. We think we are communicating, but without the proper infrastructure, the message is not getting consistently heard. Communication is the responsibility of the sender and not the receiver. As the sender of information, I am the one that needs to understand how to deliver the information in a way that makes sense to the receiver. If you look at sentinel events across the country, one of the fundamental findings in most of them is a failure to effectively communicate. That makes the concept of communication very important for patient safety as well as staff morale and organizational effectiveness.

Bruce Tulgan is one of the leading authors on leadership as it relates to the various generational segments and the way the various segments need to be communicated to. It is not uncommon in a work environment today to have four different generations represented. With the unstable economy people are also retiring later, so communication is challenging when attempting to reach everyone. Tulgan emphasizes the need for leaders to understand the preferences of a diverse population of workers. It is also important to realize that people learn in different ways, which also needs to be taken into consideration when delivering messages. There are audio, tactile and visual learners. Another concept to consider is the human attention span. So let's begin to study all these concepts and apply them to effective communication.

Attention Span

In 2000, a study conducted by Microsoft utilizing EEGs and questionnaires studied the attention span of humans to find that at that time the attention span was 12 seconds. A recent repeat of the study showed that the attention span of humans is now only 8 seconds, a drop of 4 full seconds. What is interesting is that the attention span of a goldfish has been consistently 9 seconds. You have a better chance of holding a goldfish's attention, looking at them in their bowl, than keeping your staff locked on your message. They attribute the drop-in attention span to the speed at which we receive information now and the way we multitask with mobile devices. In 12 seconds, it is barely possible to communicate a concept to anyone, but imagine trying to connect in 8 seconds. The takeaway from these findings is that an effective communicator needs to find a strategy to communicate messages in small sound bites or slogans that will resonate with the staff. Tulgan and Martin (2006), through their work, found that it takes a person an average of seven repetitions before the concept is believed. The answer then can be short sound bites over and over again. The knowledge alone of the attention span of a human can help you craft messages in a concise and effective way.

Types of Learners

There are various ways that humans learn, and most of us, depending on the way we are wired, prefer one method over another. Neil Flemming (2001) articulated various learning styles in his VARK model. For instance, I am not wired with a scientific brain. Even though I went into nursing, a science-based field, courses such as chemistry and math were a great challenge for me. When I did my MBA, finance and accounting killed me. I always enjoyed and did well in the theory classes. My daughter, however, did very well in math, and one day I asked her why she liked math so much. Her answer was because it was easy since it only had one answer and she did not need to choose. That was interesting to me because the reason I hated math was because it only had one answer and I always got that one answer wrong. I did far better talking my way out of my lack of knowledge in essay questions and papers.

Tactile Learners

Tactile or kinesthetic learning is the process of learning through touch, movement and working with your hands. It has also been found to be a very effective way to learn in scenarios where individuals need to use their hands and perform technical skills. Simulation labs are a great choice for tactile learners and especially effective in creating a safe environment for students and staff to learn from mistakes that will not harm patients. When working with tactile learners, you need to provide them an opportunity to use their hands by either taking notes, working on projects or creating mind maps. The body learns through repetition, which translates to muscle memory. Over time this muscle memory leads to automaticity and reflex actions. When I was professionally dancing, and learning many dance routines, it was impossible to think and process all the steps. It was muscle memory that made these movements automatic. I could be performing on stage and thinking of what I was going to do later, not even concentrating on the steps and yet executing them perfectly.

Audio Learners

Audio learners learn through listening. They enjoy lectures, reading out loud, doing presentations and participating in group discussion activities. These are the people that will sit through staff meetings and engage in discussions and are great individuals to put on problem-solving teams because they will engage with others. These are the staff that will use the Internet or intranet for advice or be willing to listen to taped meetings.

Visual Learners

The visual learning style is also referred to as the spatial learning style. Visual learners associate subject matter with pictures or images. They like to take notes, use graphics such as charts and graphs and prefer reading as opposed to listening. I am a visual learner. It was not uncommon for me to pick up a rental car from the airport when I was traveling. Before the era of GPS, which is great for visual learners, I would need to get a map and have the rental car employee map out my route for me in a highlighted color. If they did not do that and simply told me the directions, I was lost by the time I needed to turn out of the airport.

What is important to note from this information is that if leaders could craft their messages to meet all the learning needs of the staff, imagine how powerful that would be. A strategy to disseminate information and meet all the needs of the various learners could use a simultaneous combination of around-the-clock town hall meetings (audio), taping the town halls and placing them on the intranet for review (visual) and providing transcripts and flyers (tactile). Consider this strategy the next time important messages need to be communicated. One last grouping of concepts to consider, however, is generational differences and the way individuals from the various generations prefer to be communicated to.

Communication Expectations of Various Generations

Through the research of the previous segments, we have been building a case for a high degree of variation in the workforce with regard to communication requirements, so let's make it a bit more complicated by introducing generational differences. The four generations that we are going to cover are the silent generation, baby boomers, gen X and gen Y, commonly referred to as the millennial babies.

Silent Generation

The silent generation was born between the years 1923 and 1943, and most of them are now leaving the workforce. They were born during the Great Depression and World War II. This was the generation of my parents. They were serious and fatalistic, and women were facing some confusing moral dilemmas with regard to wanting to move into the workforce. Most women were encouraged to stay at home and care for the family. Every female who worked outside of the home was either a schoolteacher or nurse. They worked hard and complained about nothing because they grew up during the Great Depression, in an era where there were limited resources for the population. My mom spoke of eating lard on bread for sandwiches during the Depression because the high fat content helped them feel full and less hungry during the day and lard was available. Store shelves were always empty, and she remembered going hungry many times. They also had the lowest birthrate of any generation today.

From a communication perspective, they prefer their written word to be formal and direct, with appropriate punctuation and grammar. They like things communicated to them to the point, and they like information in written form to refer to later. From a verbal perspective, they are very formal and polite. They are linear thinkers and prefer that the communication is up front and to the point with no slang or foul language. They honor the chain of command and follow the policies and procedures of the company. They were also very loyal and believed that they needed to dedicate their entire lives to the company that supported them.

Baby Boomers

Baby boomers were born between the years 1946 and 1960, and many are approaching retirement at this time. They had the highest recorded birthrate of any generation. This generation redefined traditional values and moral beliefs secondary to the rebellion against the strict rules of their parents. Generational identity for this generation included things like new forms of music, rock and roll, personal freedom and the advent of social drugs.

Because they were "free," many of them planned poorly for the future and lived in a state of denial of their own demise. Those that worked were focused on money and promotion.

As far as their written communication preferences, they like information printed out and feel a paper trail is valuable. These individuals will read an email and then file it for later reference. This is exactly what I do. Their speaking preference is one of camaraderie and small talk to build important interpersonal connections.

Generation X

Generation X individuals were born between the years 1960 and 1970. This was an era of the baby bust versus the baby boomer, with birthrates dropping. This generation is known as the "nomad" generation of latchkey kids that learned to be independent and fearless. Since their parents worked and oftentimes were not home, they fed and entertained themselves, and because of their independence, their influence in society now is very strong.

Their written preference for communication is much less formal than the previous generations. They do not want to read a great deal of text. They like bullets and simply getting to the point. They appreciate a no-nonsense approach to telling them what they need to get done so they can do it. Their verbal approach is very direct with little small talk. They want to get to the point and are interested in what they need to do and how it affects them.

Generation Y

Generation Y individuals were born between the years of 1980 and 1990. They were still babies of the baby boomers, but their world was sculpted by the rapid changes in technology. They are very social, sometimes considered slackers, peer oriented and seeking immediate gratification. These are also the trophy kids rewarded for simply participating. They are privileged, demand work–life balance and are motivated by money and other tangible rewards.

Their written preference for communication is very casual, with no consideration for grammar and punctuation. Many of them have not focused on how to write in a professional manner. They prefer sort bursts of email or text for their information and will not read long documents. Their verbal preference for communication is very informal with little to no regard for the chain of command. Many have not experienced conflict due to the protective nature of their parents.

Putting It All Together

Tulgan (2006) speaks of the generational differences but, given the work environment, also has identified the notion that, given the different attributes of the various generations, when together, everyone seems to want the same things. For instance, if the gen Y individuals are demanding work–life balance, then all the employees want this same advantage. With regard to communication, the answer is to present information in several formats, repeated several times in smaller, digestible sound bites.

Communication Infrastructure

As I mentioned before, effective communication is one of the greatest illusions in any organization. We think that we are getting our message out, but without a sufficient infrastructure for communication, as well as a way to measure the results of the communication, we do not know for sure. This can lead to safety gaps in organizations. The following will be a comprehensive plan for the evaluation and creation of an effective communication infrastructure that can be modified to fit into any organization.

Objectives of a Communication Plan

Any effective plan begins with a set of objectives. Here are some objectives for an effective communication plan:

■ Analyze the current communication patterns of the organization.
■ Provide a consistent methodology for the management of communication throughout the organization.
■ Provide standards and expectations of leaders for communication.
■ Provide a template for meeting agendas and minutes.
■ Provide education for various aspects of communication.
■ Provide a process for the evaluation of the effectiveness of communication.

Once the objectives are established, development of the plan becomes organized and easy. The more inclusive the plan, the better accepted it will be by the staff. They should be engaged and asked about what are the best ways they feel they should be communicated to.

Flow of Information

In my consulting experiences, I have found that when you see one organization, you have seen one organization. There are, however, some common pathways for communication that are similar in most organizations. There are several directions from which communication and information can flow from the various levels in the organization to the staff. Figure 4.2 is an example diagram that identifies the various levels of leadership and the subsequent sources and routes of information. These may be different in your organization, which is why you should conduct your own study and fill in your own blanks. This is an example from a hospital, but it is pretty adaptable to any organization.

The center grouping of boxes shows the various levels of how communication begins its travels from hospital administration at the highest levels of the organization. The information in the various boxes that align with the first row shows where the communication comes from. As you can see, there are leadership meetings, publications, other committees, electronic formats and gossip. Yes, gossip. We will discuss this in depth a little later. This information is shared by hospital administration to the next level, the administrative team. The information is then shared by the administrators to the next level, then the next, before it gets to the staff. The message also will change from the top as it moves through the organization, for a couple of reasons. I call it "information distillation" and "information drift."

Information Distillation

A great deal of information is not going to be appropriate to share in its original format, so that information needs to be distilled into exactly the message you want to share. What is important with this delivery is that all leaders are aligned and present the information in the same way. Scripted talking points, sound bites and appropriate images will help with effective messaging.

Information flow to staff

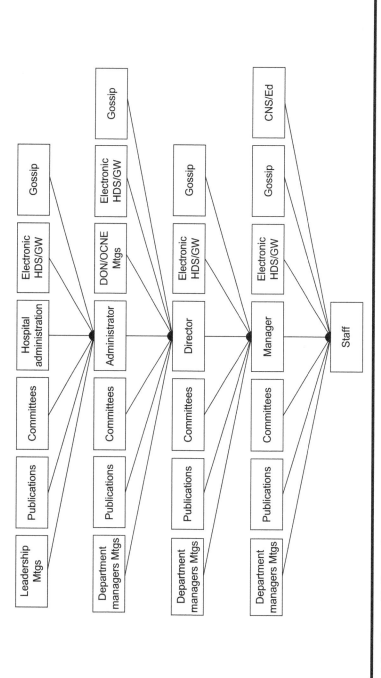

Figure 4.2 Flow of information.

Information Drift

There is an effective exercise to demonstrate information drift, and it is especially effective to try this with your team to show them how this works. We all hear things a bit differently, and we all pick up information that resonates with us, which is what we will remember. Start with a short story that one person needs to memorize and have them whisper that story to the next person, who then needs to tell the next person and then the next person until the story travels through the whole group. The last person then tells the story out loud for the group, and at that time you read the original story to show how the content drifted through the various interpretations. This is especially fun to do with kids. Their great imaginations really drift. What is important to remember is that information will change to messages that we may not have intended. There needs to be a continuous focus on the quality of the messages as they travel through these pathways.

Gossip

Eder and Enke (1991) defined *gossip* as evaluative talk about a third party who is not present but virtually included in the discussion. When we hear the term *gossip*, it oftentimes has a negative connotation that what is being said about the third party is mean or damaging. Shawne Duperon (2016), in her research on gossip, supports the fact that most gossip is actually positive, but people have the tendency to focus on negative speak. Think about it, when you talk about anyone that is not present, it is gossip, but for the most part it is positive. You speak about the good work of a team or a coworker or you do a positive evaluation about someone you work with. You talk about someone's new haircut or about someone's successes and it is positive.

An effective leader can build trust and share information through the use of positive gossip. This is an excellent way to build your team and make people realize that you appreciate them and others. The problem with leaders and the use of gossip is when the information is negative and maligning. This destroys trust and makes people wonder what you say about them when they are not in the room. Information is powerful and sends a message to the staff that you trust them by sharing information. Just make sure it stays positive.

Chain of Command

Chain of command is a very important concept to understand and follow. A simple definition of *chain of command* is simply the order of authority and power in any organization. The effectiveness of chain of command was discussed by Henry Fayol (1841–1925), who described that the more clear cut and defined the chain of command is in an organization, the better the chance that communication will be effective and decision-making will be enhanced and efficient. What is important to note about chain of command is that decisions should be made only by those who have responsibility for those decisions. If leaders usurp the authority of the leaders under them and make decisions at those levels, they destroy the credibility of their subordinates. We see examples of this all the time. A staff member is angry with the decision of their boss and wants to manipulate that decision by going to the person over that individual. When this happens, the more senior leader in this situation needs to send the staff person back to deal with their direct boss to give them the opportunity to fix the situation rather than riding in on their white horse to fix it for the staff. Open-door policies do not mean that you are there to fix things, but rather to give advice on the next steps that need to be followed.

The diagram shown in Figure 4.3 represents an example of an appropriate chain of command for information from the staff member to their manager and back to the employee. The titles may be different in the various departments; however, the concept of chain of command is consistent. You can use this type of diagram and replace the appropriate titles to fit your own organizational structure.

Communication Standards

Leaders need to make sure that they set clear standards for behaviors of all their leaders with regard to visibility and communication. In my experience, communication processes in many organizations are all over the map, depending on what the various leaders feel they have time to do. I agree that leaders need to be empowered to develop their own processes; however, they may not know what is effective without some direction or coaching. It takes a collective effort to move an organization in the right direction. Here are some recommendations for communication standards:

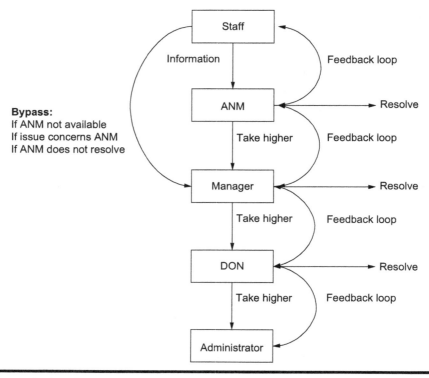

Figure 4.3   Chain of command.

- Monthly staff meetings should be conducted, with personal minutes put in mailboxes or distributed through whatever electronic platform is available to the organization.
- Monthly staff empowerment meetings should be conducted, with minutes taken.
- Regular focus group meetings (at least annually), defined as groups of three or four staff members, should be held to provide the opportunity for employees to discuss problems with their respective director/manager.
- In my hospital, I make it a requirement that directors, managers, assistant managers and supervisors will work shifts in the department to help identify with the problems experienced in the work environment. This should be done quarterly and include off shifts—this does not mean that the leader will take an assignment if not oriented to the area, yet they need to be visible and listen. Good bosses are interested in experiencing the challenges of their staff so they can fix them.
- Process improvement and general information or huddle boards are to be created and maintained in all departments to keep data visible to the staff.

- A designated location for staff to receive mail should be identified.
- Town hall meetings should be conducted, with directors in attendance, at least quarterly.
- All managers should define and communicate the appropriate chain of command for their unit/department.

What Should Be Communicated?

Along with communication standards, it is important for all leaders to understand what needs to be communicated to the staff so that all staff throughout the organization will be privy to the same information. The following are suggestions for what should be included in information to the staff, although this will vary from organization to organization.

- Appropriate information from department manager meetings
- Customer satisfaction scores
- Departmental metrics: Operations, quality
- Information from service line meetings
- Recognition
- Policy and practice changes: Safety, process, equipment
- Corporate plans: Changes in facility, manpower, compensation
- Department/unit goals/objectives and progress
- Committee meeting minutes
- Input exchange prior to decision-making
- Empowerment model information, both local operating unit and corporate level
- Department leadership meeting information
- Compliance information

Value of Feedback

Feedback is a critical factor in successful communication techniques. Ignoring a request of a staff member, colleague or other leader, or delaying a response, may send the message that their concern is not important to the manager. Here are some recommendations for feedback standards:

- Feedback must be given with every request to the leader.
- Feedback should be given within 24 hours or as agreed upon by the two parties.

- Feedback should be given verbally unless agreed to be communicated in another fashion by both parties.
- Feedback must be confidential.
- Feedback represents an inherent respect for all persons involved.
- Feedback should be given by the appropriate person following the proper chain of command unless informed by the manager that feedback will be given by another person (Figure 4.4).

Formats

Lastly, formats are important. Minutes, agenda and other publications distributed by the organization need to include vision, mission, logos, customer care models or slogans that bring the staff together and provide a constant reminder of the valuable work they do. The organization should create templates for all in the organization to use so that the look is consistent and the alignment is apparent.

Application to Practice

So, what does this mean to the phoenix leader? It is important for the leader to take a critical and analytical look at the communication practices throughout the organization and be willing to make changes when possible. What should be reviewed are the communication pathways in the organization. How do people communicate and are there any standards? What is being communicated and is this done consistently? How responsive are

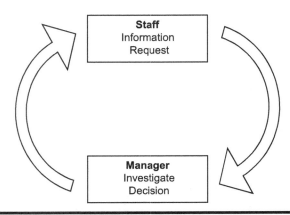

Figure 4.4   Feedback loop.

your leaders with regard to respecting the staff through feedback practices? Effective communication is the one key element in improving quality, service, staff satisfaction and processes throughout the organization. After this review, it would be valuable to get your team together to work on a comprehensive plan that is consistent, solid and designed to communicate effectively to all.

Chapter 5

Attributes of the Phoenix Leader: Building an Empowered Workforce

The best way to find out if you can trust someone is to trust them.

Ernest Hemingway

Bass (1990), in his early research and writings on effective leadership, described transformational leadership as the sharing of governance by the leader and the followers. This approach to shared decision-making provides the foundation for an empowered workplace where employees can actually contribute to their work in a meaningful way, thus increasing engagement and pride in their performance. Empowerment transforms the staff, and thus transforms the leader. Using the phoenix leader metaphor, this renewal and growth is the cornerstone to effective leadership. The transformational approach to leadership that empowers staff is recognized as the most effective approach to use with professional staff that are independent in their practice. Magnet recognizes transformational leadership as one of the major tenets of the review process for Magnet designation and vital to successful healthcare organizations (ANCC, 2014). This chapter is designed to guide you to the creation of an empowered workplace that excites and engages the staff.

Empowerment Defined

Empowerment can be defined as the practice of sharing information, rewards and power with employees. This practice allows them to take initiatives and make decisions to solve problems and improve service and performance in their own work environment. This needs to be coupled with the practice of providing the employees with the skills, resources, coaching and ultimate authority to contribute in a meaningful way. This also needs to be aligned with the appropriate structure for accountability and responsibility for the outcomes (Price and Price, 2012). Price and Price identified four major categories important to staff in an empowered environment. I will adapt all these concepts to the work environment.

1. How they work and the processes employed
2. Where they work
3. When they work
4. How they complete their work

How They Work and the Processes Employed

The only people who really know the processes at the point of service are those who are working at the point of service. Leaders continue, however, to feel that since they worked the environment at some time in their careers, they know what is going on at that level. Not true. Despite processes, policies and procedures, employees oftentimes modify their work to fit their situations or preferences. Production pressures and lack of resources can also contribute to this scenario and create what I call "the rub" that the staff learns to live with every day. This rub is not optimal; however, they have learned to work around it and over time to accept it as the way it is. Some of these altered processes can lead to safety concerns and mistakes. If given the opportunity to analyze and change their environment, the staff can easily identify these concerns and develop strategies to create the appropriate system and forcing factors that will improve the efficiency of the workplace and improve quality and safety.

Within my role as a chief nursing officer (CNO), I make it a practice to wear scrubs on a regular basis and work the units with my staff. It is amazing to see some of the issues that they are dealing with that you would never know without experiencing it. Seeing the rub allows you to take steps to eliminate the rub and improve efficiency and staff satisfaction. In my consulting experiences, I have oftentimes heard from leaders that they at times go to work in their organizations undercover to see what really happens when employees are not being "watched." My recommendation is to work in the areas but not in an undercover scenario. You have far more value if your employees get to see you working with them to really learn their challenges. You have the opportunity to show them you care about them. Don't waste this time undercover.

Where They Work

The cosmetics, layout and amenities of the work environment are very important to the staff. With regard to new construction, the staff should be heavily represented in the decisions of layout, support space and employee areas. Not all organizations have the latitude to create new construction; however, even in older organizations, cosmetic changes can greatly improve the look and feel of an area. In my experience, we created an acute care for the elderly (ACE) unit in one of the oldest and least desirable units in the hospital. We were able to carve out a section for video monitoring, which greatly decreased falls, as well as work with finishes that are appealing and safe for the elderly. These finishes included padded vinyl flooring; ambient lighting to reduce sun downing and confusion; increased safety equipment, such as railings and safer bathroom fixtures; and finishes that resembled home more than a hospital. The staff was included in all these decisions and the outcome was one of success for the patients and the organization. This refresh amazingly made the unit look new and made the staff feel great that they were part of something amazing. Any facility that is going to be upgraded or created needs employee input. They are the ones that will let you know what will work.

When They Work

Martin and Tulgan (2006) identified a variety of expectations of staff depending on their generation. What was interesting to note, however, was that in their research, regardless of the generation, when one person was given an advantage, all employees wanted that same advantage. The younger generations were those who focused on work–life balance and were very concerned about their quality time and desired more control over when they worked regardless of the expectation of the organization. Their desires have now become the expectations and desires of the entire workforce. Since this has become so important for the staff, how does a leader provide this advantage without compromising the needs of the organization?

In my first role as a manager, I experimented with the staff doing self-scheduling, which was not heard of at that time. Since we were a 24/7 operation, appropriate staff levels were vital, especially on the off shifts where additional support was absent. At that time, organizations were more command and control and driven from the top of the organizational chart. I utilized a team approach to work with the staff to develop a self-scheduling process that was acceptable to all. First, the staff needed to learn about manpower budgets and what was acceptable with the human resource processes in the organization. The outcomes of this initiative were nothing short of amazing. The following is the list of advantages realized with their self-scheduling process:

- Balanced staffing levels
- Improved staff satisfaction
- Decreased call-ins and attrition levels
- Decreased turnover rates
- Fewer complaints to me about staffing
- Faster turnaround time for feedback and vacation requests
- Balanced manpower budget
- Increased support of each other for switches and coverage for time off
- Staff also took the initiative to cover call-ins and personal requests for upcoming shifts.
- Staffing is one of the most labor-intensive roles of any manager. The fact that this was managed by staff provided me valuable time to pay attention to quality and service and other issues demanding attention.

How They Complete Their Work

In my experience, one of the biggest concerns of staff has been the desire to do the best job they can in the safest way for the consumers. Processes to reach this goal are very important to them. As mentioned before, they also are the ones who have perfect knowledge of what needs to be changed at the point of service. The same holds true when it comes to the selection and purchase of new equipment and systems. Despite the importance of their opinions, oftentimes the staff is not included in these purchases. I have seen organizations that have purchased entire new technology systems without the appropriate people involved in the choice, let alone the staff. Empowering the staff means to find ways that they can be included in all purchases that will impact them at the point of service. Once the purchases have been made, the staff should also be involved in the implementation of systems and introduction of new products. This means that staff have a say even though they may not get their way. In the event that a different choice is made due to cost or consistency, they will understand the reasons behind the decisions.

Leader's Responsibility in Building an Empowered Workforce

Empowerment does not just happen even if the leader has a transformational style of leadership. There needs to be a comprehensive infrastructure that supports empowerment at all levels through the organization and is supported by all leaders at all those levels. This leadership alignment seems to be the most difficult to accomplish with all leaders with various styles and experience levels. Another phenomenon that I have seen is the fear of some leaders that making the staff responsible for decision-making could minimize their value in the organization. This is not true. Conversely, when empowered staff improves quality and service, the leader is ultimately responsible for the outcomes and receives the recognition for those successes. The first step to an empowerment infrastructure begins with alignment of the leadership team and how they work together to begin to build a framework for accountability that will lead to empowerment. The following are necessary steps to begin this framework. Collins (2001) identifies such inspirational leaders as level 5. All organizations need to employ only level 5 leaders to get them to their desired success.

Set Expectations

Since the leader is the one responsible for the culture in the organization, the entire staff must understand what the expectations are in order to fulfill them. This should include operational issues; that is, if the staff is going to do self-scheduling, they need to understand the expectations surrounding budgets and staffing methodologies. The staff should also understand their responsibility and the expectations in relation to satisfaction and quality scores and their ability to enact strategies to improve them at the point of service. Setting expectations provides the initial roadmap on which other decisions and strategies can be created. It is virtually impossible to hold people accountable if they don't know what the expectations are that they are accountable for. Once expectations are set, then they can be held accountable for their actions.

Define Responsibilities

Along with setting expectations, staff need to understand what their boundaries are with regard to what changes they can make in their work environment. For instance, a process change in one area of the organization that is desired by the staff may need financial support or the support of other departments for the new process. The staff need to understand who are the leaders that they can reach out to for financial support or who can help with the connectivity with other departments. The staff may be interested in recommending changes to benefit packages and other human resource processes, but in the absence of collective bargaining, they will need to understand that this is not an area for them to focus their efforts. Allowing the staff to work on recommendations that they have no power to affect will demoralize them and make them wonder why they are even trying.

As far back as the times of Abraham Lincoln, visibility and approachability of the leader has been the key to the development of trust in the staff. Phillips (1992), in his book *Lincoln on Leadership*, related Lincoln's leadership success to his strategy of "leadership by walking around." Especially during turbulent times during his leadership tenure, Lincoln felt that his presence provided a feeling of safety and support for his soldiers and staff members and allowed for dialogue that not only helped him make better decisions but also elicited the support of the staff for those decisions. Quint Studor, founder of the Studor Group, in his publication *Hardwiring Excellence* (2018), supports visibility through structured and consistent rounding with the staff as a way to increase communication with them, improve the level of accountability at the point of service and provide an opportunity for real-time support and recognition.

However, leaders that feel overwhelmed with the responsibilities of their positions may find it difficult to make the commitment to consistent rounding and a high degree of visibility with the staff. The evidence from the

Studor Group positively correlates both consumer and staff satisfaction with rounding and leadership visibility. By focusing on visibility, other problems are resolved, actually resulting in more time for the managers, not less. It is difficult to achieve this realization in the managers. They need to see it and feel it to believe it.

I will kick this visibility up a notch from Studor and present my strategy. Another extremely effective way to increase visibility and trust with the staff is to set the expectation that leaders will actually work with staff in their areas. I mentioned this previously as one of my personal strategies to get out with my teams. This will provide the leader with hands-on experience of the challenges of the work area and provide an opportunity for casual dialogue with the staff. The farther away from the point of service the leader is, the less "expert" they are at processes that are taking place. The staff members are the best resource for recommendations for improvement. Of course, leaders must walk the talk and effectively role model their expectations.

Understand Your Staff

In order to provide an effective and successful work environment for the staff, the leader must know what that looks like to the staff. The only way to understand what the environment needs to look like is to get to know the staff. Although the leader sets the underlying culture, it is important to craft an environment that allows for optimal staff satisfaction and effectiveness. To understand the staff, the leader needs to get to know their staff. High visibility, an effective communication structure, staff meetings and focus group meetings with two or three staff members at a time are strategies to increase connectivity with the staff. It has been my experience that in smaller groups, people are more likely to share. Larger groups have a tendency to be dominated by individuals that like to talk, which shuts down the introverts. It is easy for the leader to manage conversations in a small group where everyone feels that their message has been heard. My recommendation is that these focus groups are conducted annually and touch all the staff. I ask one question in these meetings to keep it positive and innovative: "If I could create a work environment that would make you never want to leave this organization, what would that look like to you?" The next step is to take these recommendations and utilize them to create processes to improve the environment. If you do not act on them, the staff will not trust you and feel that you really did not care about their recommendations. The same holds true for surveys. If you utilize surveys for information gathering, you must share the data and, more importantly, act on it.

Encourage Knowledge Sharing

Especially in this highly technical world we live in, many staff members possess a high degree of academic preparation and the desire to learn and create. Sellman (2011) described several core values inherent in these types of workers across the globe. They include care, compassion, altruism and a desire for knowledge. Since these careers are science-based professions, it would make sense that a thirst for knowledge would be important. The utilization of an evidence-based approach to quality improvement would provide the foundation for knowledge exploration, sharing and risk-taking.

Encourage Risk-Taking and Innovation

Once the foundation of trust has been built between the leader and the staff, the willingness to take risks can be encouraged. In a safe environment, staff will feel that their ideas and creativity can be shared and evaluated with an open mind. The leader needs to openly encourage this level of risk-taking and help the staff to think of changes to process in new and different ways. General George Patton said, "Never tell people how to do things. Tell them what to do and they will surprise you with their ingenuity." I have personally witnessed this magic myself, over and over, in a variety of scenarios.

Empowerment in the Work Environment

Kanter (1977) studied the importance of empowerment in relation to how people react in the work environment or the situation that they are in. People become uncomfortable when their world is out of control, and if that situation is the work environment, it leads to disengagement and turnover. Especially with highly trained professionals, the need is even greater for them to control their work environment in order to deliver safe and effective service. This is the case in most modern organizations. Employees will feel empowered in a structure that provides them a voice in what they do, and that leads to an environment that enables them to work effectively. This is also critical to safety and quality in the organization, which are so important to providing successful products and services.

Effects of Empowerment on the Workforce

There are many studies and articles on the positive effects of an empowered work environment, so I have compiled them here. They include the following.

Organizational Trust

In my experience, trust is the hardest thing to earn but the easiest thing to lose. One of the findings of the literature on empowerment is the improved organizational trust between the staff and the leaders. This trusting relationship begins to build a bond between the leader and staff and begins to build an ambiance of calm that truly relaxes the staff and lets them be their best. The staff needs to know that we have their back and are there for them. This level of trust also enhances the communication between all parties and encourages creativity and innovation. I believe that every suggestion from the staff needs to be considered and appreciated, which opens the door for more innovation.

Improved Work Satisfaction

There is great competition between organizations for competent staff, and in the future, secondary to the anticipation of the increased needs of the future, the demand will increase for competent workers. Satisfied workers don't leave their jobs and are more engaged and committed. This work satisfaction also leads to a higher degree of engagement. The literature strongly supports the relationship between engagement and an empowered workforce.

Organizational Commitment

The Gallup Organization (2016a) has done more than 30 years of research on organizational commitment and the positive effects of engagement on organizations. The following is their latest release of information:

■ 87% of employees worldwide are disengaged.
■ 70% of U.S. employees are disengaged.
■ 30% of U.S. employees are engaged and happy with their workplace.

- Companies with increased employee engagement scores outperform their competitors by 147% in revenues.
- Women are generally more engaged than their male counterparts.

These findings paint a grim picture of the status of engagement in the workplace and demonstrate the important but difficult work that needs to be done by leaders. The phoenix leader can change this through effective leadership.

Enhanced Financial and Workforce Metrics

The manpower budget of any organization is the largest and, unfortunately, where most of the unnecessary money is spent. Agency utilization, premium pay, bonuses and overtime are oftentimes needed due to high turnover and vacancy rates. Improved employee engagement reduces turnover rates and vacancy rates and reduces the costs. Engaged workers are also more amenable to strategies to reduce costs in other areas and are willing to look at their contribution to the solvency of the organization.

Improved Quality and Safety

Consistency in practice is very important to maintain the quality and safety in any organization. Disengaged staff, transient agency utilization and a high percentage of overtime increase production pressure and decrease consistency of practice. In my experience in healthcare, increased falls, medication errors and infection rates have been associated with organizations with disengaged staff. Poor service and poor product productions can be identified in other industries. The endless pursuit of quality needs to be priority one for any leader. This is our work. This is what we do. This is our calling. If we are not able to do well in these areas, we are failing, yet organizations across the country continually struggle with these challenges.

Customer Satisfaction

Have you ever heard the phrase "If mom isn't happy, no one's happy?" Literature suggests that if the staff isn't happy, the patients won't be happy. Research conducted in Magnet healthcare organizations strongly supports this notion. Aiken et al. (2009) articulated this research in several publications. This is another area where the managers need to focus time that they think they don't have, yet they will receive an incredible return on this investment.

Building an Infrastructure for Empowerment

So how do we achieve the amazing outcomes we just discussed? By building an effective empowerment infrastructure. There are several success factors necessary to build an effective infrastructure for empowerment in any organization. These success factors will inculcate the culture of empowerment and begin to build trust with the staff. Three of these factors are a supportive organizational administration, transformational leaders and a formalized empowerment infrastructure (Gokenbach, 2007a).

1. *Supportive administration*: There is no way to build an empowered work environment without the staff feeling supported and trusted by senior administration. The flavor of the sundae starts at the top, and if the culture of empowerment begins there, it is easier to cascade through the organization. There also needs to be an expectation from senior leadership that all members and disciplines in the organization communicate, deliver and support each other. The absence of such leadership will lead to a unilateral approach that fails to engage the entire organization and leads to a disjointed approach to care delivery.
2. *Transformational leaders*: As previously discussed, transformational leadership is the most effective approach for highly skilled professionals. All leaders in any organization need to be transformational. The reason to focus on this specifically in this segment is secondary to the fact that in any organization, manpower is the largest cost with the most contact with the consumer. Workers at the point of service are also the ones that are there around the clock to provide continuity of service. The challenge is that all leaders need to embrace and learn to lead from a transformational approach. At all levels of the management structure, leaders need to be coached and educated on the behaviors of transformational leaders. Leaders need to be open to the recommendations of the staff and willing to allow them to be innovative and improve their environments.
3. *Formalized infrastructure*: Lastly, it is important to create a comprehensive infrastructure that presents a pictorial model, vision, bylaws and operational structure that can be understood by the staff. This will

depend on the size of the organization and whether there is a corporate structure in place as well. The most effective strategy for developing this model is to include the ideas of the staff and others that will be affected by the operation of the model. I have worked with the staff to create several different empowerment models, and they all have been a bit different based on the structure, size and needs of the organization. Creating a unique structure designed by staff and supported by leaders is the best scenario for success.

How to Begin the Construction of an Empowerment Infrastructure

Throughout my consulting experiences, I have had the opportunity to work with a variety of organizations to help them develop their empowerment infrastructure. There is not a "one-size-fits-all" empowerment structure for every organization. The underlying theories will be the same, but the model will need to fit the organization. Size, resources and corporate structures must be considered prior to the creation of your model. There are, however, steps that can be followed in a systematic way to begin the process.

1. *Understand the vision and mission of the organization*: Regardless of the strategy for any initiative, it is vital to understand the mission and vision of the organization and to align the structure to achieve the organizational goals. It is important to not only use this as the building blocks to your model, but also connect the dots for the staff as to its importance. All work achieved by the staff will help contribute to the goals of the organization. If the organization has an effective and well-developed model for quality and service, that becomes the bedrock of the empowerment model. In the absence of a coherent model, one needs to be created and adopted.
2. *Conduct a SWOT analysis*: Conduct a SWOT analysis of your department to understand what strengths, weaknesses, opportunities and threats are currently present. For instance, a strength could be strong support from senior leadership, while the opposite would pose a weakness or threat. A good deal of trust between the leaders and staff could be either a strength or an opportunity, while a lack of trust could be a threat preventing the effective rollout of the structure. Once the analysis is conducted, there may be strategies that need to be employed prior to

the success of the empowerment structure. It is important throughout the SWOT analysis to be completely honest with the state of the organization as it is. It is recommended to organize a team that is willing to be honest to help with this analysis. In my experience, I have seen senior executives that are blind to the current state of their organization and unwilling to see themselves in the context of the issues. The SWOT analysis also needs to include the input of the leadership team.

3. *Designing the retreat*: There is tremendous evidence that supports the notion that staff input greatly improves the likelihood that staff will support the strategy. The best way to effectively create this model is to bring the staff and leaders together in a formal way to strategize together. I like to use the concept of a retreat, which sounds positive and less threatening to the staff. I know that many organizations may feel that this is expensive and not necessary; however, it sends a powerful message to the staff that they are important and their input is vital. It is important to have a significant number of staff members in greater numbers than the leaders so that they do not feel that their suggestions will be overshadowed by those with more authority or minimized by that authority. The following is a list of the categories of individuals that I have used in the past in healthcare organizations; however, given your organizational structure, you will have a different mix of individuals that you need to include based on the particular makeup of your organization. Here is the mix of staff for a healthcare setting:

Myself, the CNO	1
Nursing directors from every division	5
One manager from every division	5
One nurse from every unit	24
One educator	1
Assistant nurse managers	2
House supervisors	2

Total leaders = 14; total staff = 26. This is an almost 2:1 representation.

You may also have some other categories that you would like to include if you have them in your organizational chart. This model can effectively be used with any department or organization by substituting the appropriate membership.

The next step is to develop the agenda for the day. I recommend that you give yourself enough time for brainstorming and strategy development.

4. *Agenda and retreat activities*: You can design your retreat in any way that you see fit, but I have always included some elements that have been very successful to align the attendees and create the environment where they feel that can be creative and share. These are shared below.

Icebreaker: There are many icebreakers that will help get people laughing and aligned and feeling more relaxed in the environment. There are actually books available for icebreakers. Choose one that fits well with the attendees.

Objectives: It is important to set the stage with the objectives that you will accomplish by the end of your time together. Be as clear as you can so that everyone is aligned with your thought processes. Taking a large group of staff off for a significant amount of time is a great financial and time commitment. It is important to pack the day and be successful in the achievement of all the goals.

Brainstorming: Take some time to brainstorm. Ask for the elements that they want to see and what they would like to achieve with the new empowerment model.

Design the model: Once the group knows what they want to accomplish, it is time to design the model. This would include elements such as

a. Frequency and length of meetings
b. Membership
c. Standard agenda
d. Utilization of appropriate rules and structure
e. Reporting relationships
f. Processes prior, during and after meetings
g. Follow-up on issues
h. Communication strategies

5. *Bylaws*: Bylaws will become the bedrock for the building of the infrastructure following the work at the retreat. Bylaws will take time to create, so it is not practical to think that coming up with them will be accomplished in the short time of the planning retreat. It is more

beneficial to develop a team to work on the bylaws offline and then bring them back to the group for input. It is also possible to look at various bylaws from other organizations who would be willing to share with you. Utilizing a model for bylaws will allow you to simply insert the information specific to your model and customize your approaches.

6. *Rollout campaign*: One of the most fun and important components of the creation of your empowerment model structure is the marketing and rollout campaign. It is critical to the success of the model, to make sure that every staff member in the organization understands the model, their role in the process and the importance of their communication through their councils. This should be a very visible and fun series of events that have a variety of communication modalities, including printed materials, town halls and presentations, information tables and a whole host of other strategies. This is a great opportunity to allow the staff members to develop this campaign since they will have the best insight as to what would resonate with the staff. It is also important to include communication to other members in other departments and all ancillary departments as they need to be aligned.

7. *Elections*: Selection of the first members of the council is critical to its success. Ideally, these members should run for this office on their units and be selected by their colleagues. In my experience, this has been most successful if the staff interested in the chair of their unit-based councils submit a letter of intent including why they would be a good choice in this selection, and the voting is then based on the information in the letters.

   Unfortunately, in the beginning of this process, there may be a great deal of skepticism among the staff, resulting in lack of voluntary submissions. In this situation, it is appropriate for the manager to identify someone that they feel is a leader and would be able to carry the responsibility of the work and to explain to them how important their talent will be to this program. I have heard from some nurses that they have been "voluntold" that they need to be involved rather than have volunteered. This is usually a short-term problem because when the council is up and running effectively, and the staff sees the excitement and success, people want to be involved with the winners and candidates begin to surface for the next election.

Once the council has been elected, the next step is to pick a chair and cochair. The process is the same with letters of intent and the voting being conducted by the members of the new council. As the senior leader, I was interested in getting the team started off in the right direction, so I was always the one to conduct the first couple of meetings until the chairs were in place and functioning. I then began to pull support and let them take over.

8. *Constancy of purpose*: As with any significant change, this will not be easy. The keys to long-term success are to realize the challenges, work to build trust and maintain a strong constancy of purpose. At this time, it is critical to support the group and encourage them to continue the work. It is always better to begin with smaller, easier projects that will provide high visibility and appreciation from the staff and quick wins to profile their value. This will begin to build trust between the members and the staff at large. I am the type of person that wants to see successes quickly, so at times I need to take a deep breath and focus on the concept of "baby steps," which means that as long as the process is moving forward, that is an indication of true success. There is a great deal of learning and growth that needs to take place, but once that happens, *if supported by leadership*, the team will take flight.

   Notice that I italicized the phrase "if supported by leadership." This support is critical to the success of the council. The council needs to be led but not dictated to. They will need to learn to process situations and may make some mistakes along the way. This is fine, and it demonstrates growth. Responsibility without the necessary authority will frustrate and diminish the work and spirits of the staff. With that said, there are areas that this council will not be able to affect, such as corporate structures, payroll and benefits, but that should be clearly delineated in the bylaws, and the staff need to understand why those things may be off limits. In reality, they are oftentimes off limits to those of us in leadership positions due to corporate structures, so they should spend their valuable energy on improvements that they can own.

9. *Evaluate effectiveness*: Building a strong empowerment model infrastructure in my mind is a quality improvement initiative. As with any process improvement plan, there needs to be an ongoing evaluation of the progress that includes input from the members and then making changes to modify or improve the approach. Probably the one issue I consistently hear from staff when there is a new model

is that the leaders are not always supportive or convinced of the value of the council. You may want to keep this in the back of your mind to proactively watch for evidence of nonsupport in your leadership team.

Review of My Most Successful Model

I have effectively utilized empowerment model structures since early in my career, before they were even identified as valuable. I met Timothy Porter O'Grady in the 1980s when he came to speak to our organization on empowerment. I was hooked. I always valued his visionary insights and until this day have used his knowledge as well as personally connecting with him as a colleague and mentor. I utilized this council for more than empowerment; I also incorporated a leadership training program within the context of the meeting, so the council became my "farm club" and most of my new managers were hired out of this team. The following are the important and effective tenets of my model.

Overview of the Comprehensive Model

To begin with, every unit was required to have a unit-based professional nurse council (PNC). The expectation of the unit-based PNC was to meet monthly to discuss issues that were important on the floor. The unit manager was not part of this group but was invited when necessary. The chair of the unit-based council was required to meet regularly with the manager to discuss the recommendations and begin working on strategies to improve. The work of the unit-based council was also presented at the monthly staff meetings to inform and solicit more ideas. The managers were expected to meet regularly with their council chair and provide support and recommendations.

The chair of the unit-based council attended the monthly hospital PNC. At this meeting, the unit-based chairs had the opportunity to present any ideas that could advantage the entire organization as well as work on strategies at this level.

If there is a corporate structure, the chair of the hospital PNC represents their hospital at the system-based PNC that has membership from leadership and PNC chairs from every organization. At this meeting, strategies are shared and adopted by the system, but it is also an opportunity for leaders to filter information and receive recommendations from staff for issues at the system level that would advantage all organizations.

Membership on the Hospital PNC

Members included one nurse from every unit that also functioned as the chair of the PNC. These were all voting members. Of this group, the chair and cochair, who was also the chair-elect, were also voting members. Other voting members included an educator, advanced practice nurse and any other nurse from ancillary departments that wanted to be included and felt it was valuable to them. Nonvoting members included one director who was appointed and rotated out every year and one nurse manager who was elected by the PNC. We also included one of our legal staff, who was a nurse and who was very helpful with the creation of documents and policies. As vice president and CNO, I had a great presence on the PNC but was not a member. My hospital president, my chief medical officer (CMO) and myself presented organizational updates monthly. We also solicited ideas and recommendations from them.

Rotation of Members

Rotation of members was always difficult because what we found was that the members truly enjoyed the work and did not want to rotate off. They were allowed to be reelected to another term if their unit staff decided that. Fifty percent of the staff rotated off each year to try to maintain a fresh look with new members. We titled them Cohort 1 and Cohort 2. The members each had terms of 2 years. The first year they were Cohort 1, and the second year they became Cohort 2. We also required mandatory attendance so that if someone missed two meetings, they rotated off and a new representative from their unit was elected.

Reason for Cohorts

As I mentioned before, one of my goals for the PNC included the development of leaders that could move into key positions in the organization. To this end, we created a didactic program of leadership development and training that was part of every meeting and also included continuing education credits. Members of the PNC were asked what competencies they felt they needed to be effective, and leaders chose the rest. As members moved to Cohort 2, the courses were concentrated on more advanced leadership and management skills.

The courses were presented in the first half of the meeting for 1–2 hours, depending on the extent of the content. Experts were chosen from within the organization to present these topics. Other experts were invited from local universities and organizations to present the rest. We did offer continuing education units for all the presentations.

Monthly Schedule and Standard Agenda

I felt very strongly that if this PNC was going to be considered valuable, there needed to be a significant time commitment. One of the concerns I hear over and over in organizations is that in many situations the manager would keep the staff on the unit due to workload, so they felt they were not supported by leadership. To eliminate this concern, the PNC met monthly for 8 hours and the staff were not scheduled in the clinical area for the day. The members were also given 4 hours a month at the discretion of the manager to complete their work. It was the expectation of the managers that these 4 hours would be granted within the month. The PNC met 10 months out of the year, forgoing July and December for holiday considerations. The agenda was created as a framework for consistency and visitors were invited as necessary.

Framework for the Agenda

- *Introduction and approval of minutes*: This was handled by the chair and in the absence of the chair, the cochair.
- *Leadership update*: This was my time to present to the PNC to provide updates and receive recommendations. Along with me was my hospital president and CMO, who also had the opportunity to provide information and solicit recommendations from the group.
- *Visiting guests*: It became the practice in our organization that no decisions would be made in other departments without the input of nursing if those decisions would impact nursing in some way. This time was allotted for representatives from other departments to either give updates or solicit recommendations from nursing for potential changes in processes. This became difficult to manage over time since the PNC became very popular and an important source of vital information. We

did notice, however, that news processed in other departments was more effective due to the direction and support from nursing.

■ *Education component*: As previously outlined in the section above, Cohort 1 and Cohort 2 would split into two rooms for their respective learning opportunities. This lasted 1–2 hours based on the programming.

■ *Lunch*: Following the educational component, all members would break for 30 minutes for lunch and return for the afternoon sessions.

■ *Problem identification and small group work*: The bulk of the afternoon was focused on problem identification and small group work. Members were allowed to choose the projects that interested them and utilized this time to develop strategies to address. Following this work, all members met back together to present their work and solicit recommendations from the rest of the group. The leaders in the group were responsible for helping the PNC identify appropriate individuals that needed to be contacted for the changes, as well as identifying resources to help them with their work. In corporate situations, this work is what would be presented to the system council. In the absence of a system structure, these strategies were presented to what we called the Nurse Executive Leadership Team (NELT).

Problems and recommendations can come to the council in a variety of ways. Staff on their units can identify issues to be presented to the larger group. Leaders in the organizations can identify projects that they would like the council to work on. Topics of conversation can also come from the corporate level to include input from the staff at the bedside.

Outcomes

Whether in my own organizations or in organizations that I have coached through this process, many positive outcomes have been identified. From a qualitative perspective, members felt that they were listened to and their feelings resonated with the staff throughout the organization. They also felt that they were able to be creative and take risks, and that they positively contributed to their work environment.

The topic of my doctoral dissertation was focused on the quantitative measures of empowerment model intervention. These outcomes were studied in the emergency department and manifested as reduction in attrition, reduction in turnover rates, decreased vacancy rates, improved nurse satisfaction scores and improved patient satisfaction and quality scores. Financial indicators were also positive as there was a reduction in vacancy rates, which eliminated agency use and severely decreased overtime and orientation costs of new staff. Quality indicators also improved, but this was not part of my study.

Your Model

Of course, your model will be designed around the needs and structure of your organization, coupled with the vision and desires of the staff and leadership. Feel free to be creative and unique. The only requirement is that you meet the intent of the vision and that vision is aligned with the organization. Figure 5.1 is an example of a model that was created utilizing the above-mentioned strategy at Greenville Health System in South Carolina. This model represents a corporate structure with all hospitals aligning under one corporate leadership council. It is important, however, in large systems, to not forget the power of the unit-based council since that is where the ideas will begin.

Application to Practice

The phoenix leader is focused on renewal and innovation and is not afraid to let go of old practices in favor of new ones. With regard to empowerment, the phoenix leader is also not afraid to allow those around them to be

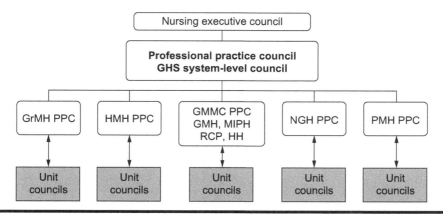

Figure 5.1   Example of an empowerment structure.

successful and, more importantly, recognized for their success. An effective empowerment model infrastructure has the capacity to provide for great organizational success shared by many. These concepts of change and innovation relate to both scenarios: the creation of new and exciting models, but also to the need to refresh and rebuild infrastructures that no longer provide the outcomes or never did provide the desired results. If you do not currently have an empowerment model infrastructure, you need to create one, but also, if your model is not working, create a new one and rise out of the ashes of the old. Evaluate your current structure or begin thinking about the creation of a new strategy. Your staff will be appreciative of your efforts, and this will be a great quick win for you and your leadership team.

Chapter 6

Attributes of the Phoenix Leader: Interdisciplinary Team Leadership

> The great leaders are like the best conductors—they reach beyond
> the notes to reach the magic in the player.

Blaine Lee

No leader can accomplish great things alone. The reality is that the role of the leader is to lead teams to success and then allow them to enjoy that success. Simon Sinek (2014) writes that leaders should have a higher purpose of taking care of the team first. He further states that organizational successes and failures are clearly a result of leadership when many individuals still believe that it is managerial acumen that is responsible. These are two different competencies. The leader needs managerial acumen; however, they will not be successful without superb leadership and the ability to move teams to success.

Serena Richards (2015) echoes these thoughts but also states that effective leaders help their teams understand their contribution to the overall goals and mission of the organization and how that involvement will lead the organization to success. I call it connecting the dots for the staff. We oftentimes tell staff what we need them to do, but we fail to tell them why. It always frustrated me when I asked my mom why I had to do something and she answered, "Because I said so." I truly did not understand the meaning behind the task, which made me more resistant to performing it. We in effect do this to our staff if we don't let them know the value they bring to the organization through their work. With regard to team leadership, that alignment is critical to effective change.

Team Defined

There are many definitions of the concept of teams, but all of them surround the notion of a group of individuals coming together on the same side to accomplish a goal. Sports teams align with the goal of winning the game. We celebrate these wins when our favorite teams are successful; however, when our teams are successful in the work environment, that is also winning and should be celebrated as well.

Another concept that is becoming increasingly important is the value of formal multidisciplinary teams whereby members from different professional positions come together with varying specialties and expertise to improve the quality of healthcare in organizations. This approach is focused on the elimination silos in organizations that are detrimental to alignment and communication, and so vital to safety in the delivery of products or service. The complexity in the healthcare industry underscores this issue. The Department of Health and Human Services (2016) recognizes a multidisciplinary approach as vital to quality and safety in healthcare organizations. This approach is also applicable to other industries, especially on the global stage. Koszyk (2013) describes this approach as building a community of experts focused on important teamwork centered on the consumer. As healthcare continues to become more challenging and complex, the melding of these specialties is required to accomplish goals. Regardless of the scenario, the theories and expertise around leading teams are the same and can be applied to any scenario. An effective team leader has a grasp of these theories and possesses these competencies.

Tyler Reagin (2016) identified 10 characteristics of effective team leadership:

1. *Leveraging influence for the team*: It is important to be the beacon of light for the team and represent them well to senior leadership. It is the team that will get the recognition, but oftentimes it is the leader that will need to secure support and resources for their accomplishments. In light of economic pressures on modern organizations, this representation is vital.

2. *Approachable*: Leaders have to have effective communication skills with a high degree of emotional and social intelligence. Possession of these skills will make the leader approachable. Especially in the team environment, there needs to be effective dialogue that will only be transparent if the leader is open to varying beliefs. During team sessions, the leader must never criticize the recommendations of the members, but rather listen and support a healthy discussion of the concepts.

3. *Solid grip on reality*: I am a firm believer that everyone's reality is different based on their values and other inherent differences. With regard to reality, it is important for the leader to understand their perceptions in the context of the work with the team. I have observed teams that were ineffective secondary to the leader refusing to look at the reality of the situation and continuing to attempt to drive the decisions in a particular direction despite the inability of that direction to achieve the results.

4. *Relational*: Great team leaders are experts at managing relationships within the team. Especially as the team moves through the stages of development, relationships can be strained, potentially threatening the future of the team. Particularly when working with diverse teams, perspectives may be very different and at times not easy to align.

5. *Consistent*: Have you ever worked with someone who was inconsistent with their behavior to the point that you did not know what kind of day you were going to have with them in the work environment? Of course, you have. It is one thing when it is a staff member that everyone learns to tolerate or stay away from, but when it is the leader, the environment becomes tense and chaotic. As a team leader, this type of individual will maintain an environment of unrest and undermine the trust of the team and prevent progress toward the goal.

6. *Calm and stable*: The reverse of inconsistency is vital to a nurturing team environment. Just as a calm and stable household is important to the successful growth and learning of the family, it also is important in the team environment. Stability fosters innovation and risk-taking and allows for forward movement.

7. *Release ownership and delegate*: I have seen this as one of the most difficult competencies for leaders who are not comfortable with their role identity. Leadership is less about doing and more about leading. Micromanagers and those that are uncomfortable trusting others will stifle the movement of the team. We will discuss delegation in a comprehensive way later in this chapter, but at this time it is important to remember the value of effective delegation.

8. *Self-awareness*: We have spoken about the importance of self-awareness to effective leadership. It is also very important in the application of teamwork. There are always challenges working with teams, and it is important to understand how your feelings may contribute to certain situations so you can manage your responses.
9. *Trustworthy*: Trust is one of the key foundations for organizational success. A highly principled leader will be appreciated by the staff and will engender faith in the team to move forward and increase the drive to achieve the goal.
10. *Respected*: Lastly, a trustworthy leader will garner the respect of the team. It is also important to remember that respect is a two-way street. It is critically important for the leader to reciprocate with trust of the team in order to receive it.

Stages of Team Formation

The formation processes of teams have been studied over time by many theorists. There is a consistent model of progression of teams as they come together. In the beginning, teams will not perform well despite the homogeneous nature of the members. Bringing together individuals from varying backgrounds will add another more challenging element to team evolution.

Bruce Tuckman (2016) in 1965 released his model of team performance as teams move through predictable and detectable stages toward success. These stages are forming, storming, norming and performing. Later, he added another stage, which he calls adjourning. It is important to understand these phases as well as the leadership behaviors to effectively move them to the next stage.

Forming

This stage is characterized by excitement and awkwardness as new team members begin to get to know each other and learn about the charter of the team and the work they will be doing. The leadership responsibility at this time is to take a highly visible role that manages the discussions and presents the vision and mission of the team and the goals that need to be accomplished, as well as helps team members get to know each other. Icebreaking activities can be fun and effective during this stage. This is also the time for the leader to present the charter and expected behaviors of the members of the group. The length of time this stage will take depends on whether there is familiarity in the group that allows people to align more quickly. It may take longer with diverse teams. The leader needs to be patient as the leader continuously moves the team forward.

Storming

The storming phase of team evolution is the most tenuous but one of the most important. It is the time when most teams will fail due to a high degree of frustration coupled with a low degree of trust. The forming stage creates boundaries, whereas the storming phase is the time for breaking through the boundaries. Members may become less "polite." Conflicts arise and individuals fall into their preferred mode of operation, which may not align with that of others. Goals, strategies and ideas are challenged, and members begin to challenge authority and emerge in importance above other members.

It is critical at this time for the leader to first understand that this is normal and also to be ready for it to occur. This is where leaders need to be calm and consistent in their approach, yet firm in the management of unacceptable behaviors. It is important for all individuals to be heard since this can be the stage where introverts or shy members will shut down and not contribute, leading to frustration and feelings of inadequacy. Brainstorming and nominal group processes are great ways to ease the team through this tenuous time. Leaders that have the skill to effectively manage this phase will end up with a powerful, aligned team that is poised to do the work.

Norming

Instability in the storming phase is what is responsible for the movement to the norming phase. Team members now know each other and learn how to handle each other's emotions and behaviors. There may still be episodes of storming; however, they will not be well tolerated by the other members of the team who now feel empowered.

The leadership strategy for this stage is to reward good behavior and support the team as they begin to move forward with their goals. At this time, it is important to provide guidance to the team on an ongoing basis and help them realize their value to this work. Encouraging a high degree of socialization also helps to bind individuals together.

Performing

This is the most productive and fun phase of team evolution, where individuals now have aligned with the goal and are moving forward. Ideas are formulated and discussed and strategies are created and implemented. Team members feel comfortable with each other and are not worried about interpersonal conflicts since these have been resolved in the prior two phases. This is the time for the team leader to delegate appropriate tasks all the while providing support and positive feedback, as well as gratitude.

Adjourning

Tuckman more recently added this last phase to team formation that he termed adjourning. This will be more pronounced in teams that have been brought together for certain project work of a delineated timeframe and more intense if the team has been successful and taken ownership of their work. They don't want to leave it behind, and they will miss the comfort and camaraderie of their team members. Tuckman likens this to mourning over a loss. Longer-term teams, such as leadership teams that have expected prolonged working relationships, will not experience this unless there are leadership changes that are coming.

The leader's behavior at this time is to understand and support the members as they grieve. It is important to highly profile the work to allow the team to see the value of it and to receive recognition for their commitment and excellence of work. It is also important to build a legacy for the team members so their work can be recognized. Plaques with their names on it or naming a program after them may help to build pride and ease their sorrow. Recognition events at the end of the work can also be helpful. It may also be valuable to invite them to become involved in other teams working on more projects.

Other Leader Responsibilities

We have touched on many of the leader's responsibilities with regard to effective team leadership, but I wanted to expand on a few concepts that I believe require more discussion. These are team selection, orientation of new members, the art of delegation, measurements of success and celebration.

Team Selection

One of the most important strategies for team success is putting together a coherent and talented team. Utilizing the goal of the team as the foundation, team members should be chosen for their expertise and energy that can be applied to the work. It is important to select a variety of team members from varying backgrounds and styles to provide quality input.

Various abilities of the team must also be taken into consideration. You will want experts in the discipline, but don't forget other components that will be needed, for instance, someone who is strong in data and analysis, someone who is strong in process improvement and strategy formation and individuals that are creative thinkers. It is also critical to make sure that the members of the team do not match the character and desires of the team leader. Diversity is what will provide a better, more robust product at the end, although it may create more challenges during the storming phase. If the leader chooses to select only members that are like her, she may just as well make the decisions herself. This also provides more exposure to group-think since there will be no one to challenge the decisions.

Orientation of New Members

Just as you onboard new staff to their roles, the leader must effectively onboard the team members to the team. It is important during this phase to align everyone under a common vision and mission and to outline the specific goals of the team. Ground rules should be established for attendance, behaviors and meeting structure.

One of the keys to creating a cohesive group is to create a sense of community among the members. Give them a chance to get to know each other as well as let them know why they are there. For instance, if you have selected someone strong in data since that will be a component of the work, make sure they know how valuable their role is, as well as that of all the members. The same is true for all members and what they will uniquely provide to the team. If the leader notices that there are individuals that are not feeling connected, it is important to reach out to them and engage them to solicit their thoughts. I remember one of my greatest leaders and mentors doing this to me during a leadership team meeting. It was a regular leadership meeting of all directors, but for some reason I was unhappy that day and not myself. I was not contributing and decided just to get through the meeting without being noticed. My chief nursing officer (CNO) noticed my behavior and said to me in front of the team that I was not myself and she was missing my usual valuable contributions to the team. That recognition gave me pause and called out my behavior in a nonthreatening way, and it also made me feel that my contributions were valuable and missed. That was the last time I was disengaged through a meeting. She is still a great friend and mentor today. I will always appreciate that coaching on her part, which is another illustration about how simple actions and moments by a leader can last a lifetime.

Art of Delegation

There are many definitions of *delegation*, but I happen to like the *Merriam-Webster* definition, which is "the act of empowering others to act." Empowerment is exactly what we have been discussing in most of the chapters in this book, and the act of delegation, if done properly, can grow and empower the staff. If not done properly, the converse it true and it can destroy or demoralize the staff. We are going to discuss my thoughts on successful delegation based on my experiences. Remember that there is a fine line between the terms *delegation* and *dump*. You never want your staff to feel that you are dumping on them.

Advantages of Effective Delegation

The following are the advantages that I have identified for effective delegation.

Delegation Extends Your Productivity

I have repeatedly said that no leader can do it all. Delegation can extend your productivity by providing a way to get more work done through the talent of others. It is important that work should be done by the appropriate level of staff. Leaders that continue to work at levels below their position are not only wasting their time but also sending a message to their staff that they don't trust them. Delegate to the appropriate staff who have the skills and give them a chance to excel.

Delegation Empowers People

I have heard over the years from many leaders who find it hard to delegate to subordinates that they feel bad about delegating and giving more work to others, so they just do it themselves. The converse is true. Delegating can flatter the staff and engage them in ways that no other strategy can if done effectively.

Delegation Can Grow People

Delegation can help to grow people by increasing their experience base and providing them visibility in the organization. This is a great opportunity to profile those leaders on your team that you want to potentially promote in the future or those that are part of your succession plan. Your staff in these positions will appreciate the opportunity to do well in the organization, which will also increase their level of loyalty.

How to Delegate Well

Delegation can help develop skills in the staff, but if not done appropriately, it can lead to demoralization of the staff members as well as loss of valuable productivity and time. The following are strategies to help you delegate well and develop your staff.

- *Define the goal succinctly*: The goal of what you want the team or individual to accomplish needs to be very clear. Give them time to ask questions and help them understand exactly what the goal is. This does not need to be prescriptive as to what the evolution of the product will look like, but the outcomes need to be clear.
- *Select the right person or team*: Make sure that the individual or team you are delegating to has the skill to accomplish the work. There will be learning throughout the process; however, you need someone who knows how to navigate the systems that will be needed for the outcomes. If it is a staff-level person, make sure that they have a mentor or backup person to go to for advice throughout the process.
- *Ask respectfully*: The way that you recruit the people you want to delegate to is critical to their engagement in the process and their level of joy with their work. When asking them to help you, describe why you

need their help and explain that you chose them because you honor their inherent talent. If you do not make them feel valuable, the delegation will feel more like a dump of work. Connect the dots and let them know that you value them and appreciate what they have to offer.

■ *Solicit their thoughts and views*: If you are not interested in the staff's thoughts and views, you might as well just do the work yourself. Solicit their ideas early in the process. This will give you the opportunity to coach them more effectively on what you need from them, but it will also give you the opportunity to visualize the product you will receive from them. This step can help you improve the quality of the outputs.

■ *Give authority, time and resources*: In my opinion, there are two major mortal sins that leaders can commit with regard to their subordinates. One of them is usurping their authority in front of their staff, and the other is giving responsibility without the authority to do the work. The latter is what I will discuss at this time.

■ If you trust someone with a vital responsibility, you must give them the authority to do the work. There is nothing more frustrating than not having the authority to get the work done. This approach will hamstring the individual and make them feel that they are doing all this work for nothing. I have had experiences in my past with certain leaders that have done this to me, and my frustration trumped my learning and feelings of ownership with the project. Give them the authority to get the work done and move those barriers that may limit their authority.

■ The other commitment that you need to make when you delegate to your staff is to give them the time to get the work done during work hours. If the project is important enough to you, then it is important enough to carve out the time. Let the staff know the timeframe and the amount of time you will provide for the work, then stay true to your word.

■ Lastly, you must provide the appropriate resources; these may be a financial commitment, equipment or supplies. Whatever they are, make sure that the team has the resources at their fingertips so that the work can progress.

■ *Get out of their way*: Once the team or staff understand what they need to do and in what timeframe and you have given them the resources they need, get out of their way. This is your opportunity to continue to build their trust by setting them free to do their work.

■ *Schedule follow-up checkpoints*: As you create your timeline to complete the work, make sure to agree with the staff on when there will be checkpoints to ensure that they are moving along. This is not designed to be a punitive, check-up-on-you approach, but rather a time to make sure that the team is getting all the support they need to help them move forward. This is their opportunity to discuss challenges and solicit advice from you.

▪ *Evaluate and support throughout the process*: Effective leaders are there for their staff and have an open-door policy and high visibility. The same is true for your team. Make sure that you are accessible to them whenever they need your support so they don't feel that they have been left drifting at sea.

To quickly recap our discussion, delegation is a valuable tool for the leader to extend their work and develop their staff. It must, however, be done effectively in order to provide the highest degree of value possible.

Measurement of Success of the Team

There are two components of measurement to demonstrate the success of the team: objective and subjective. The objective components will provide the data that demonstrate achievement of the goals. The subjective component will provide individuals to comment on their feelings of progress.

Objective Measurements

Prior to the start of the work that the team will engage in, objective measures need to be identified as ways to measure success. These indicators may be financial in nature or dedicated to the measurement of quality, safety and service. With value-based purchasing, much of the teamwork in hospitals at this time is focused on the Hospital Consumer Assessment of Healthcare Providers and Systems (HCAHPS) scores, throughput, infection rates, readmission rates and nursing quality. Other industries have their own unique set of metrics that need to be followed. There needs to be a comprehensive plan on what type of data will be collected, how and when it will be reviewed and what the target measure for success will be.

Subjective Measurements

Oftentimes the inability to produce the objective targets has to do with problems with the subjective measures. What I mean by this is how the team is getting along and how the members feel about their contribution to the work. It is important that this be measured after every meeting in an anonymous fashion to provide the leader with insights as to how the meeting can be run more effectively or how the members are personally feeling about the process. I created this meeting effectiveness tool that is to be completed and turned in after every meeting. It is anonymous in nature so that there is no fear of reprisal. The leader will be able to glean from this information what changes may need to be made in leadership strategies or even potential changes in team members. Figure 6.1 shows an example of the meeting effectiveness tool that I have created and used very effectively.

Title of Meeting: _____

Date:_____   Time:_____

Leader of meeting:_____

	YES	NO
The meeting was well run		
The objectives were obtained		
The meeting ran on time		
The leader managed the group effectively		
All members had the opportunity to participate		
I found this meeting valuable		
I felt my contribution was valuable to the team		
I feel that the team is on course with our goals		
Comments:		

Figure 6.1   Meeting effectiveness tool.

Celebration of Success

Celebration is a very important component in our lives. We celebrate weddings, birthdays, graduations and other successes. Celebration brings closure and recognition. I truly believe that in our healthcare organizations we take so much for granted and don't celebrate our successes enough. For instance, if you stop to think about the fact that we all contribute to making lives better every day, all day, in some way as part of our regular work, that is amazing and a true gift to be able to serve in this way. We need to include celebration whenever we can, and the conclusion of the work of a team is a great opportunity to celebrate success and recognize the staff that participated. Make this work as visible to the organization as possible, so that the recognition is greater than the team members and the leader.

Virtuoso Teams

I wanted to present the concept of virtuoso teams since this approach is a way to quickly achieve innovative results. Virtuoso teams are a specially designed team of elite experts in their field and in industry that are created for ambitious projects (Fischer and Boynton, 2005). The individuals chosen for this type of team possess incredible energy and innovation and are willing to work relentlessly at a frantic pace. Virtuoso teams are considered risky and, because of the type of individuals on the team, can be difficult to manage. Because healthcare is steeped in culture and generally moves very slowly, virtuoso teams are not typically utilized; however, if you are willing to take the risk, they can pay off with great results. I have effectively used virtuoso teams in my organizations to achieve results, and I believe there is a place for them elsewhere in healthcare. The challenge with them is that the leader needs to be willing to take the risks and committed to acceptance of the strategy.

A classic example of a virtuoso team is Microsoft's X-Bot team, assembled specifically to develop a revolutionary new gaming product that would far surpass the highest-yielding product, Sony's PlayStation 2. In a very short period of time, the X-Bot team far surpassed the expectations of Microsoft and created an unbelievable product that captured the market and passed the competitors with ease. Many organizations reach beyond their own walls to bring in the type of experts they need, but healthcare organizations routinely look within their own ranks to find people that fit the criteria for this approach.

Fisher and Boynton describe the forming of these teams as similar to the process of assembling conventional teams with a few differences, including the following:

- *Assemble the stars*: In traditional teams, the focus is on choosing people that are interested in the project but also have the time to devote to the goal. In the virtuoso strategy, people are chosen specifically for their talent regardless of their familiarity with the scenario.
- *Build the members' egos*: Superstars generally have high egos. In the virtuoso approach, the focus is less on the collective good of the team and more on what the individuals bring to the table. They will work on components of the project in a solo capacity and need to feel good about what they bring to the table.
- *Make this work a contact sport*: This is about working fast and furious and generating ideas. The focus is on creativity and conflict. Ideas need to be generated and discussed with transparency and energy that at times may hurt the feelings of others. Members of this team cannot take things personally but rather must focus on the goal in lieu of their feelings.
- *Address the sophisticated customer*: Programs designed by this team should be designed to delight and surprise the customer, thereby separating the organization from all other competitors. With the high degree of competition in healthcare, it is important to deliver well above the expectations of those we care for.

I have had success utilizing the concepts of virtuoso teams and I have found these individuals to be fun and exciting to work with. To apply this concept to your own organization, however, requires the leader to set the stage for their success. The strategies that I have used to this end include

- Soliciting buy-in from senior leadership to support the process
- Notification to all appropriate departments of the process and strategy, along with the importance of this approach
- Communication of specific timelines for the completion of work
- Communication of what will be needed from others to support the work
- Communication of data and success on an ongoing basis
- Expression of gratitude to all who supported the process
- Celebration that includes the team and those who supported the team

Application to Practice

The concept of the phoenix lends itself to creation. No leader accomplishes anything on their own, but rather with the efforts of their team. It is important for leaders in this context to do a critical review of their success with teams and the success of their leaders in the way they lead their teams. First, do all leaders have a sound understanding of the theories of team leadership and their effectiveness? Do they understand the concepts of effective delegation? All these concepts are easily taught. It would be a good exercise to conduct a formal evaluation with the creation of a strategy to improve team leadership. Also, become familiar with strategies for managing multidisciplinary teams since they are vital to success in healthcare.

Chapter 7

Attributes of the Phoenix Leader: Change Agency

We are chameleons, and our partialities and prejudices change place with an easy and blessed facility, and we are soon wonted to the change and happy in it.

Mark Twain

When I ask managers what is their primary responsibility as an effective leader, I get all kinds of answers, from fiscal responsibility to human resource management to strategic planning for the future. Of course, all these responsibilities are components of the role of a leader; however, the fundamental responsibility is that of change agency. If you think about it, what leaders describe as their role cannot be accomplished without effective change leadership. The concept of the phoenix is about the ability to change and renew and, more importantly, inspire their staff to change as well. This chapter focuses on the fundamental concepts of change, along with strategies to improve this important skill.

Change Agency Defined

The term *change* can be easily defined as becoming different (Merriam-Webster, 2016a). We as human beings are actually very good at change. We grew up, went through many milestones in our lives, may have gotten married or divorced, had kids, changed jobs, went to school, experienced personal loss, moved and made large purchases in our lives, all representing our ability to effectively deal with change. After 40 years of observing leaders and staff in the workplace, I find that the fear of change comes from two major concerns, fear of the unknown and loss of what is familiar, both of which create feelings of being out of control of one's life. The effective change agent understands this.

IMPACT Greensboro (2011) defines a *change agent* as an individual who understands the concepts of change as well as the dynamics that surround the concept. Change agents also know how to identify what needs to change, assess the readiness for change and then effectively implement and sustain the change. They describe that to be an effective change agent, one must understand the concept of collective community. Collective community in the context of change means the understanding of the fear factor associated with change and methodologies for allaying these fears in the staff.

George Couros (2013) identified five characteristics of effective change agents. Here are my translations of his characteristics:

1. *Clear vision*: You don't start driving to a new destination without a clear knowledge of where you are going and how to get there. The same is true with any change. The vision or direction must be clear so that the team implementing the change knows where to go and, most importantly, what they need to do to get there. I have seen many leaders fail because they did not set the direction and clearly represent the expectations with the ultimate goal.

2. *Patient yet persistent*: As I have mentioned before, culture is a powerful force against any change, and people will do whatever they need to do to protect the status quo. It is important to remember that you only need 20% of the staff to engage in the change to begin to move the group in that direction. I use the concept of baby steps, engaging people one at a time until the critical mass is achieved and the tipping point is reached. I have seen leaders become tired and frustrated with the slow movement, to the point where they give up and walk away from the change. Continue to look at the endpoint and not the barriers because there will always be barriers.

3. *Ask the tough questions*: This skill is important not only in change but also in any scenario. I find asking the tough questions to be especially helpful when trying to understand a situation and scenario. Ask the question in a safe and caring way that does not alienate those around you.

4. *Knowledgeable and lead by example*: The leader should definitely be knowledgeable of the situation to engender trust in the staff. It is important to realize that this does not mean that the leader has perfect information about everything involved in the change, but they should be willing to engage the experts who can provide that perfect information. Leading by example is also important in any aspect of change. Show the staff that you are with them every step of the way and are willing to personally do what you are asking them to do. I remember early in my career as a nursing director that our chief executive officer (CEO) decided to cut costs in the cafeteria. Hours were cut, which left many staff without any option for food, and many of the products were eliminated that he felt were too expensive to provide. What the staff noticed, however, is that this CEO never ate in their cafeteria but rather ate with the doctors in the private dining room, where no changes were made to the menu and, in fact, the products were of a higher quality. This was always contested by the staff, who had little respect for much of what he did. It seemed like some small changes in food items should not be so profound; however, these seemingly small decisions in his mind damaged respect for him in a bigger way.

5. *Strong relationship based on trust*: As I have said many times, trust is the hardest thing to earn but the easiest to lose. Staff that truly trust their leaders will be more amenable to change, trusting that their leader has their best interest at heart.

Types of Change

Another important component of successful change is the type of changes we are faced with and understanding the differences between them. Although the steps to manage the change can be similar, the speed with which we accelerate the change may need to be different. I identify these as evolutionary, forced and invented change.

Evolutionary Change

Evolutionary change is the change that happens over time. This can be defined as the natural progress through life that we experience on a daily basis. The progression is slow, so oftentimes the observable changes are not noticed in real time but rather over time. In the context of our lives, this is what is expected; our kids grow up and leave the nest, and we grow older and hopefully wiser. In an organization, however, this evolutionary change can signal stagnation and the inability to meet the demands of a changing environment due to the evolutionary strength of the culture. We see this in organizations that have not had much leadership change over time. The culture becomes extremely strong, resulting in resistance to change. From a relationship perspective, strong alliances form between staff, to the point where the addition of new staff members becomes challenging because they are not accepted into the community.

The strategy to deal with these types of organizations is oftentimes to change out the leadership team in lieu of new ideas and approaches. If you are hired into this type of organization, the approach needs to be one of working to understand the culture prior to the establishment of any change strategies. It is key in this type of scenario to spend a great deal of time with the staff and work to establish a base of trust. Inclusion in the change process is important, so that the staff feels they have control over their environment. Unfortunately, if the organization is so resistant that it is clear the change will be difficult or impossible to achieve, more members of the team may need to be changed.

Forced Change

Those of us who have been in leadership positions long enough have probably had the experience of forced change. Many of the forced changes we have seen have been secondary to financial challenges leading to organizational changes or restructuring. The challenge with forced change is that there is not always the time to develop a comprehensive strategy that will be effective and accepted by the staff. If organizational leaders continue to respond to environmental forces prior to them becoming a crisis, they should be ahead of the curve and in a position to execute planned change rather than chaotic change. This change provides the highest level of anxiety on the part of the staff because they are generally not included in any of these decisions, but rather need to wait for the outcomes and the unknown effects they will have on them.

Three ways to help prevent forced change are

■ Always review the organizational structure for scope and reorganize.
■ Always review every open position before filling it.
■ Don't wait for financial challenges to become a trend—react immediately.

Invented Change

The last category of change I like to call invented change. My definition of *invented change* is the type of change that all leaders should be engaging in on a continual basis. This is a proactive rather than reactive approach that responds to the demands of the environment. One of my greatest mentors told me that to keep your organization open and responsive to change, you need to continually provide opportunities for change. Over time, the staff becomes comfortable with change and begins to trust that their lives can be better through change. This type of change also allows for the greatest degree of staff involvement and innovation. It builds an infrastructure for an empowered workplace. This change also keeps the organization's deliverables fresh to the consumer. Early on, when I was big in fitness, I owned a gym. One of my approaches to keeping clients interested was to institute a new program or bring in a new piece of equipment on a monthly basis. There was always the next challenge for them to look forward to. Apple is spectacular at this ongoing change with the hype of the newest iPhone far before its launch.

Change Theories

It has been my experience working with leaders that those who are effective change agents apply some science behind it in the form of change theories and models. There are many types of models and theories that refer to physiological change and personal readiness for change, but for the purpose of this discussion, I will present what I have found to be the most effective change models. Over the years, I have perfected my own model that focuses on empowerment as a large component, so I will present that as well. Kristonis (2004) profiled the change between all the theories.

Lewin's Change Theory

One of the most recognized and utilized theories of change is that of Kurt Lewin—a social scientist who believed that human behavior is a delicate balance of various forces that oftentimes are in conflict with each other. This conflict is what has a tendency to create resistance and stagnation. He identified three necessary components to change.

Unfreezing is the first step in the process, which means challenging the status quo. Lewin believed that there were driving and restraining forces that maintain the equilibrium in an organization. In order to unfreeze, the leader must either increase the driving forces or decrease the restraining forces, which will open the door to change. This could be described as presenting the negative outcomes of not changing or the positive outcomes of what the change will bring.

The second phase is change whereby the leader introduces the new process. It is in this phase that behavior needs to change, which will require the leader to engage the staff and move them to their new reality. Staff needs to be supported at this point and resistance addressed.

The last phase is refreezing, where the change is now inculcated and becomes the new reality. It is very uncommon that change will be sustained without a focus on refreezing. It is common for individuals to revert back to their comfort zone and reverse the effects of change.

This model is very simplistic because it does not take into consideration all the minute components inherent in these phases. It does, however, provide an overall framework for change.

Lippitt's Model of Change

Lippitt et al. (1958) created a more comprehensive model of change that expanded on the work of Lewin but filled in the gaps with steps that are the responsibility of the change agent. The seven steps are

1. Diagnose the problem.
2. Assess the motivation and capacity for change.
3. Assess the resources and motivation of the change agent. This includes the change agent's commitment to change, power and stamina.
4. Choose progressive change objects. In this step, action plans are developed and strategies are established.
5. The role of the change agents should be selected and clearly understood by all parties so that expectations are clear.
6. Maintain the change. Communication, feedback and group coordination are essential elements in this step of the change process.
7. Gradually terminate from the helping relationship.

The model of Lippitt et al. is more comprehensive and provides more direction through their articulation of actual steps to follow. Their philosophy focused on the need for the change agent to commit to approaching change more collectively with support from the greater organization.

Kotter's Change Model

John Kotter (1996) is one of the leading researchers in the area of organizational success. Since his original publication, *Leading Change*, he has studied organizations utilizing his eight-step process for organizational change. His model is based on the fact that the world is moving at a much faster rate than in the past, but our ability to keep up with the rate of change is not increasing in speed. This is true in the healthcare environment, and the complexity of the healthcare industry further complicates the issues. Kotter's model includes the following steps:

1. Create a sense of urgency.
2. Build a guiding coalition.
3. Form strategic vision and initiatives.
4. Enlist a volunteer army.
5. Enable action by removing barriers.
6. Generate short-term wins.
7. Sustain acceleration.
8. Institute the change.

   Kotter's model is comprehensive in the actual creation and institution of change; however, one of the most important components of change is to make sure that it has been built into the fabric of the organization, so if utilizing this model, there needs to be the evaluation of success and revision if necessary.

Gokenbach's Model of Empowered Change

Secondary to all my experience leading organizations through change, I have over time developed my own approach to change that has never failed me. Because I am a great proponent of an empowered work environment, I took the liberty to call my model Gokenbach's model of empowered change (Figure 7.1). I will present all the steps and relate them back to components of other models. I attempted to make this model comprehensive and a "one-stop shopping" approach to immediately apply to any

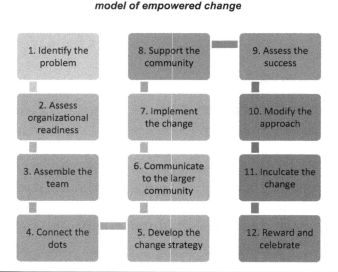

Figure 7.1 Gokenbach's model of empowered change.

change scenario. I find that defining more steps to the process provides a roadmap and helps leaders clarify some of the problematic areas of change. Here is my model.

1. *Identify the problem*: Anything I do or think of in leadership begins with fundamental knowledge and introspection. To that end, the most important part of the change process is first to identify that there needs to be a change and then what needs to be changed. This can be either reactive to a current situation or proactive, looking at better ways to provide service or create evidence. Quick identification of problems or issues that should be changed requires that leaders stay current in their quest for knowledge, aware of their surrounding environment, including competition and opportunities, and lastly, thirsty for creation. This step should include supporting data that can be compared later to measure success.

2. *Assess organization readiness*: As a leader, you will be required to institute change regardless of whether your organization is ready. That is not the problem. The reason for this step is to identify where your challenges may be and where you will need to focus attention while developing your strategy. You will need to be honest with yourself, especially if your organization struggles with change, since you will not want to understate the energy that will be needed to be successful with change;

there is also a small window of opportunity. Challenges provide the opportunity, but the leader needs to react quickly and communicate the need for change.

3. *Assemble the team*: As we discussed in Chapter 6, the quality of the team that you put together is critical to the success of the process. This also gives you the opportunity to include individuals that are close to the practice and have perfect information of the reality at the point of service. This is very empowering to the staff and results in better outcomes and more engagement on the part of the staff.

   Here is an example. Review of our linen budget revealed that our linen usage in my hospital was well above our compare group and far exceeded our budgeted allowance. Administration charged environmental services to develop a strategy to reduce linen costs based on their assessment of what they could do. They came up with the process of making beds with just a fitted sheet, draw sheet, pillow, pillow case, towel and washcloth. It was clear that this could help to bring costs down; however, the analysis showed that the results were still below target. I asked that we get a group of staff together that were stakeholders in this process to show them the suggestions and ask their input. In relation to the recommendation of the environmental team, they suggested getting rid of the draw sheets since they now use the large pads, and they didn't need to put towels on the bed since they don't often need them and could get them themselves. In addition to these recommendations, they came up with a page and a half of additional recommendations. The staff also suggested that they would be willing to develop and execute the educational plan for the rest of the staff. This not only resulted in greater buy-in from the staff, since their peers developed the process, but also began to immediately bring down linen costs.

   There will be some scenarios whereby it will not be appropriate to include staff, especially in situations of staff reductions and mergers, but I have found that there are very few situations where staff cannot be involved.

4. *Connect the dots*: If you want to fully engage your staff, they need to know the thinking and reason behind the change. I call this connecting the dots. For instance, in the linen scenario discussed above, I connected the dots by explaining to the staff the need to cut our costs and what that meant to them in relation to their annual bonus and salaries, which made it real for them and incentivized them to help.

This is also the time to create the sense of urgency that is identified as a critical element in other change models. I have found throughout my career that the more information I can give to the staff, the more they will understand. Information also represents a high degree of respect and helps to build a trusting environment.

5. *Develop the strategy*: In the attempt to provide a comprehensive model, I include this step dedicated toward the development of the strategy. An important component of this step is to do your homework with regard to research, canvassing the environment, utilizing data and acquiring input from the staff. This strategy should include not only the change but also the plan for communication, education, implementation and analysis, as well as a plan B. Alternative scenarios are helpful in the event that certain components may not be effective.

6. *Communicate to the larger community*: Communication in my opinion is an incredible art, and those that do it well achieve greater success than those leaders that don't. With regard to the communication of change, it is important to share the story effectively to the larger community to enlist their support. What is important to highlight is the team that worked on the strategy and served as the experts involved. It is also important to connect the dots for the larger community as you did for the team. What should be included in the communication is
   a. Some historical perspective on what is happening and why
   b. Sharing of data
   c. What this means to the staff
   d. The process utilized to reach the chosen strategy
   e. The implementation plan and timelines
   f. A plan for assessment of success
   g. Time to answer questions

7. *Implement the change*: Now that you have effectively set the stage for your change, it is time to implement the change. Stay true to your plan since this is the one that you designed with your team and presented to the greater community.

8. *Support the community*: Throughout any change, it is important to listen to what I call the "word on the street." Listen to the cues that will tell you how the change is going. Utilize those who helped create the strategy to provide the guideposts as to how people are responding to the change. It is my practice that I am always very visible, but in the event of change, even more visible so that I can personally ask people what they think and how I can support them. Feel free to call

forums together to discuss the change, especially if it appears that it is not working as well as you thought. Even in the event that the change is something that there is no negotiation about, supporting the staff can help smooth out the rough edges of the perception of the change.

9. *Assess the success*: In order for the change to be inculcated in the culture, it is paramount that you continually assess the progress and level of success you are having with the implementation. You only need 20% of the staff to support the change to get the ball rolling, but it is easy at this time for anyone to become disengaged from the vision if the ongoing support and assessment is not there. Set timeframes for check-in. That may be every week in the beginning and stretching that to every month if things are going well. Remember that old ways die hard and staff will have a tendency to slip back into old behavior patterns. When assessing the success, you need to look at both "soft" components, such as feelings of the staff and gossip, and "hard" components, such as the data elements that you have decided to track.

10. *Modify the approach*: The worse way to attempt to have staff buy in to change is the "my way or the highway" approach. If you identify that there are components of the change that are not going well or don't make sense once in practice, engage the staff in suggestions on how to improve that piece of work. That empowers them to share their thoughts but also makes them feel valuable. I had a situation in the past where we were charged with eliminating staff. Since this type of change does not lend itself to staff involvement, my directors and I decided that we could eliminate one secretary from every area. Sounded simple enough and was easy to execute. The units were very large, with 56 beds being the smallest and 119 beds the largest. The reason for two secretaries was simply the vast geography of the layout. Within 1 week we knew the decisions we made were not practical. Patients were complaining that there was no one to help them, doctors were complaining that they could not get anything done on the units and staff were complaining that they were now performing tasks that took them away from the bedside. I immediately apologized for the absence of judgment, reinstated the unit clerks and asked the staff for cost-cutting ideas, of which they came back with several. This move on my part truly helped to build trust with the staff and increase commitment at a tough time in the organization.

11. *Inculcate the change*: I have heard many leaders over the years share stories of how change events were unsuccessful in their own

organizations. One common denominator that I have identified in these stories is what I call the "drawback of interest" on the part of the leader. After a period of time, we assume that things are in place and we turn our attention to the other thousand things on our desks. Without continued attention and monitoring, this is the time where the staff will begin to drift back to old ways. We need to continue to reinforce the change until there is no opportunity for drift back. This may take varying lengths of time depending on the magnitude of change, but a tremendous amount of energy is spent on change on the part of all involved, so don't waste those efforts by allowing the drift back to old processes.

12. *Celebration*: I am very big on celebration. I celebrate everything with the staff because I believe it shows respect for their hard work and brightens their day. When one of my emergency departments hit their service goals, I bought them all logo jackets and celebrated with a huge pizza party. When my organization achieved their first Magnet designation, we celebrated with an around-the-clock pinning ceremony of all the staff as well as a beautiful spread of hearty hors d'oeuvres and desserts.

I truly believe that one element of success for all leaders is the utilization of tried-and-true ways to develop effective infrastructures to accomplish work. With regard to change, whatever model you choose to use, make it your own by creating a strategy that can be repurposed for every change event. I hate the cliché term *thinking outside the box* and substitute the term *innovation* instead. Thinking differently opens up many opportunities for change (Figure 7.1).

> When a company is able to identify, and pursue neglected innovation dimensions, it can change the basis of competition, leaving other firms at a distinct disadvantage.
>
> **Mohanbir Sawhney**

Innovation Defined

Merriam-Webster defines *innovation* as "the introduction of something new or the generation of a new idea, method or device." When we think of innovation in the business sense, Sawhney et al. (2006) define *innovation* as the creation of value for customers achieved by changing some dimension of the offer. In healthcare, we see a great degree of innovation on the side of products and procedures; however, we tend to struggle with innovation on the side of care delivery and efficiencies. This is where if we can begin to think differently, we can greatly improve the quality, safety and service in our care delivery. The key to success in healthcare organizations is to understand the complexity and what is needed to align and motivate individuals to change.

12 Different Ways for Companies to Innovate

Sawhney et al. (2006) developed what they called the Innovation Radar, which is a 360° view of the various dimensions of business innovation and the ways that these dimensions are related together in a circular model. They divide the dimensions into four areas: the business offerings (which represents the what), the customer (which represents the who), the business processes (which represents the how) and the presence (which represents the where). It is interesting to translate this model to the healthcare industry as in my experience, I have not seen this methodology either discussed or utilized. The following sections discuss the tenets of the model.

Offerings

Within the offerings are two components, the platform and solutions. In industry, a platform is a form of product development connecting various products to one identified brand. In healthcare, the platform would be what types of services are offered and how they are connected to the greater whole. Solutions can be defined as the solving of problems. In healthcare, this would represent all work surrounding the delivery of the product. In one of my positions, I was responsible for creating a new Gamma Knife program in radiation oncology to be used in the treatment of brain cancers and other lesions, which would be one of the few in the area. The platform was the Gamma Knife service, and the solution was all the work surrounding the development and implementation of the service.

Customer

Every organization serves a customer regardless of what they produce or offer. In my administrative experience in healthcare, it has not been that long that the healthcare industry has shifted its focus from serving patients to serving customers. To this day, however, I still see resistance in some clinicians to facing the fact that healthcare is one of the most profound service industries. The reality is that there is so much more in the offering of healthcare than simply patients in the hospital setting. Within this category, the focus is on the customer experience and value capture. Hospitals and healthcare organizations are now being held accountable for service scores, which represent the type of experience that customers are having with their service. Along with the experience, the product they are receiving must be value-added to them. I recently had a wonderful experience with a new dentist following my relocation to another state. When I arrived at the office, all of them introduced themselves and said that they were so glad that I was going to be a new patient there. I was taken back right on time and everyone there focused on me as if I was the only person in the office. Even my new dentist spent far more time with me than I thought she needed to and made me feel very important. They truly hit the mark on service, and if given a survey, they would have received all highest marks.

Value is also important. The dentist presented not only a plan for my ongoing necessary care but also many cosmetic improvements that they provide in the office. Those were very expensive and, in my opinion, not value-added at this time, so I opted for the basic dental care. Experience and value are critical to superb consumer satisfaction that leads to loyalty.

Processes

Processes are simply the way that products and services are delivered. In this category, Sawhney identified organization and supply chain as the vital components to focus on. In any industry, the organization represents how we deliver service in the most effective and efficient way. In my experience, this is the area in which many organizations struggle secondary to culture and holding on to the old ways of doing things.

Presence

Presence is simply where the services and products are provided. The two identified components in this segment are networking and branding. There are many large organizations with expansive geographic footprints. As important as the locations and footprints is what is offered at what sites. I have seen growing systems struggle with this. Mergers and acquisitions oftentimes result in duplication of services throughout many entities, creating competition within the same organization. Savvy administrators need to be very strategic as to the elimination or repurposing of some of these services. In one of my experiences with a very large hospital system, they had four women's hospitals all providing the same service, which competed against each other for patients as well as staff. It took several years for the decision to be made to close one of them that was geographically close to another. Closing or repurposing services and locations is difficult but needs to be done sooner rather than later in the product or service lifetime before negative financial impact on the organization.

Networking and branding are critical to the marketing of the organization. Especially in mergers and acquisitions, a new combined or emerging brand needs to be created and disseminated as quickly as possible.

Sawhney et al. (2006) suggest that the Innovation Radar model can provide topics on which to focus innovative strategies. Their research also has found that most organizations fail simply due to lack of focus and inertia. Focusing on focus and moving forward is at times all that is needed to improve innovation in an organization.

> Your most frequently used tool should be your imagination, not your memory.
>
> **Nido Qubein**

Levels of Thinking

Synecticsworld, Inc. (2011) is an organization that specializes in innovation utilizing innovative thought models. They identified that one way to expand the concept of innovation is to learn how to think across a larger spectrum. I use this model in my organization and in my consulting work. It clarifies the various levels of thinking and also helps to create the philosophy for safe risk-taking. They identify five levels of thinking in relation to change:

Level 1: Rational thought—When we approach problems and begin to develop a strategy for change, most of us begin with the first level of thinking, which is that of rational thought. For instance, we need to revise a process or policy so we first look at what we are currently doing, what is rational and relevant to us now. We then look to the research to see if there is anything we can add to the policy based on the latest evidence, and we revise the policy by making minor modifications. This approach allows for change, but it may be limiting to what we can do if we look at the problem with different lenses.

Level 2: Diversity—Diversity can be simply defined as a mix of various things. We think of diversity in the context of culture, race, religion and gender, but what about the application of the concept of diversity to change? This simply means to mix it up. When you approach a problem, begin to add various elements into the solution. This could be through the creation of a diverse team that think differently and come from various backgrounds with different rich experiences. Virtuoso teams are examples of diverse thinkers. In a healthcare setting, you could include individuals on the team from various departments and departments with little understanding of yours. This will provide a fresh look or diverse look into the issues at hand.

Level 3: Wishing—My grandson is the king of what I call "creative wishing." He is always developing strategies, toys, games and activities for himself that all begin with a wish, and he is always so proud of the amazing things that he creates. I am always impressed as well. He is 8 years old. Kids are masters at this, but as adults we seem to lose this edge over time. Kids have no boundaries when it comes to wishes because they have not been tortured by the barriers of reality in the real world. They simply believe and those beliefs become reality to them. Toys are designed to promote this type of creative play that expands the mind.

When you wish upon a star, makes no difference who you are.
When you wish upon a star your dreams come true.

Walt Disney

I am sure you remember this song from *Pinocchio*, sung by Jiminy Cricket, which speaks to the importance of wishes. Wishing has the potential to expand thinking and enhance creativity. One approach that has worked very well for me is asking the staff a question that opens up the potential for creative wishing. That question is, "What would that look like to you?" For instance, with regard to the work environment I would ask,

- "If this was the best place for you to work, what would that look like to you?"
- From a change perspective, the question might be, "If we could develop the best approach to this problem, what would that look like to you? If this was the most efficient process, what would that look like to you?"

The beauty of this question is that it is nonthreatening and nonlimiting in the answer and can be applied to any context. It encourages thinking and encourages people to think differently about the issues at hand. It also keeps the comments positive and prevents people from running down the rabbit hole of negativity. This format for questioning allows people to wish again. To possibly think like a child again, which is a safe place for all of us to revisit from time to time.

Level 4: Analogy/metaphor—Metaphor is a powerful way to promote a different way of thinking. It is the application of a thought to a word or phrase to which it is not literally applicable. For instance, with all my graduations from various degrees, I felt so free it was like driving a Mack truck off my chest, my metaphor for pressure. Most people who have had the experience of school can relate to that metaphor. This book is based on the metaphor of the phoenix and the ability to renew and re-create yourself. If the metaphor is strong enough, the vision of the metaphor alone can evoke certain responses. Hopefully after reading this book, the vision of the phoenix will remind you that resilience and relevance are based on your ability to be creative and self-reinvent.

I am now living in Texas. An application of a metaphor to the team might be something like "If we were the Dallas Cowboys, how would we approach this?" The Dallas Cowboys evoke certain feelings of team, winning, success and fun, so this has the potential to open up thinking along these lines. I also understand now why everyone says things are bigger in Texas.

Level 5: Irrelevance/absurdity—Now we start the fun. The highest level of creative thinking is that of irrelevance and absurdity, or creating something totally different out of something ordinary. I remember that when I was younger one of the hottest toys was a pet rock. It was nothing but a rock (totally free to most of us who looked for them) with two googly eyes glued on. They came in a little cardboard box that looked like a little cage, and some of them came with names. I actually owned quite a few of them, as well as did most of my friends. I don't think you can come up with a more absurd concept, but the inventor of the pet rock became a multimillionaire. Inventors have the capacity to habitually think at this level, which is what stimulates that unbridled train of thought. Think about all the inventions that we see in the healthcare industry. Who ever thought of putting a wire umbrella in a vessel to catch blood clots? Who ever thought about electrocuting the heart to make it beat again? All these inventions began with wild, absurd thinking that, once evaluated and honed, led to some of the greatest inventions of all time. You can, over time, improve the comfort level of this type of thinking with the staff by encouraging this type of thought process and rewarding their creativity.

I use an exercise with my teams when I want them to think differently. I have them pull out any object from their pocket or purse and ask them to create a product to sell that has nothing to do with what it is. It is amazing what they come up with, and I find that this type of exercise lets them feel free to think differently. I then tell them that in the approach to this current problem, this is the thought process I want you to use to come up with a creative solution that is different than anything we have done in the past.

I find that if we don't think this way, we continually try to change our world using the same old solutions, which I am sure you have heard is the definition of insanity. We cannot continue to look at problems from the rational perspective. I like to use the concept of the fresh look. If things are not working, take a fresh look. Blow up the past ideas and strategies in favor of the new. Think about all the issues we face in healthcare; begin to take a fresh look at

- Falls
- Service
- Infections
- Human resource management
- Safety

This approach is applicable to any industry and any improvement that you feel is important or necessary to your organization's success.

You will be effective at change if you think of change in a different context.

Cultural Competence

One of the greatest pitfalls of successful change is the culture, which can build a strong resistance to anything new and destroy the opportunity to move forward. Culture can be thought of on several levels. From a societal perspective, it is the collective beliefs, customs, arts and behaviors of a society. Culture grows stronger as it is proven successful to extend the life of the society it represents. Vincent Van Vilet (2014) describes the notion of organizational culture as "an abstract concept" whereby organizations have learned to survive based on the development of a set of beliefs and behaviors. These beliefs become very engrained and strong over time and difficult to change. To be an effective change agent, the leader needs to be culturally competent and able to understand and navigate the culture of their particular organization.

Edgar Schein's Model of Organizational Culture

Edgar Schein (2010) was a professor of business administration whose passion was the study of culture in organizations. In 1980 he debuted his theory of organizational change and the role that culture plays in organizational change. His model is based on three levels: artifacts and symbols, espoused values and underlying assumption. He also related these levels to those of an onion, where the outer layers lend themselves to change and the deeper the layers, the more fundamental and difficult to change (Van Vilry, 2013). Once a leader understands the role of culture, this knowledge can be applied to change strategy.

Artifacts and Symbols

Artifacts and symbols are visible elements of an organization that comprise the outer layer. These could be things like logos, particular colors, uniforms or dress, organizational structure and architecture. In one of the larger organizations for which I worked, the colors were burgundy and white and all the buildings were beige with the same exact angular architecture. There was a strong culture of formality with dress and behavior. There was a video that all new employees needed to watch on dress. The corporate CEO was shown with a suit on and the jacket unbuttoned, with the underlying caption reading "unacceptable too informal." The same CEO was shown in the next shot with the same jacket buttoned and the caption reading "acceptable." I actually did not see that there was much of a difference between the two photos and found it quite amusing; however, that was the expectation secondary to the cultural beliefs of the administrators. Skirts were preferred for female executives. I always wore a suit with slacks, possibly because I have always been a nonconformist. No one ever mentioned it to me.

Because these items are on the outer layer of the model, they are easier to change. When this organization acquired two new hospital systems, the logo was changed and the colors changed to blue and white. Once changed, an expansive marketing initiative was launched to introduce the new organization to the public.

Espoused Values

We discussed personal values early in this book—how they are acquired and how valuable they are to who we are as individuals. Organizations go through the same evolution of values developed in much the same way as ours. We mentioned that values come from our parents, our experiences and our environment. Within organizations it is much the same. The values of the originators of the organization are the founding values that become espoused throughout the years by the leaders. For instance, there are faith-based organizations that are closed on Sundays to allow for worship by their staff despite the loss of revenue. Academic medical centers value research and are very involved in education and research that is very expensive to support. High-tech organizations such as Apple and Microsoft value creativity and not only expect creative approaches from their employees, but also specifically hire for that skill and then create a work environment to support innovation.

Espoused values are very difficult to change and can bring disaster in the case of mergers and acquisitions. I mentioned the example in Chapter 3 of the merger of two hospitals and the problem with abortions now being performed in the hospital that prior to the merger was faith based but now no longer was. That is a profound example; however, more subtle problems arise in all the mergers and acquisitions, such as what managers will remain, what units combine with what units and how the staff react to each other.

Underlying Assumption

This is the underlying truth of the organization that is taken for granted by those in the organization. This truth is what the individuals in the organization truly believe based on their prolonged experience. Working in several different organizations as well as in my consulting experiences, I have heard over and over that "this is how we do things here." These patterns of behavior derived from the subconscious assumptions that everyone has learned to accept make change very difficult.

Steps to Effective Cultural Change

It is important to realize that culture has the power to destroy change initiatives, and simply changing a logo or leadership will not necessarily affect the change and align the staff. In all my merger and acquisition experience, I have developed my own strategy to address culture in an effective way. Here is what I recommend based on what I have found effective in my experience.

1. First, become familiar with the notion of culture. I find Schein's model very helpful to identify the elements that need to be evaluated prior to attempting change.
2. Seek to understand the culture by initially observing the organization prior to making judgments and attempting to move forward with change.
3. Understand the organizational chart, hierarchy, matrices, formal and informal structures and relationships.
4. Talk to the staff about the culture of the organization. Seek to understand their core beliefs and assumptions since they will give you great insights into potential barriers.
5. Never say things like "where I come from" or "in my experience" or especially, "this is what I think we need to do." These statements will put up barriers between you and the staff because they will feel that you do not honor their culture.
6. Involve the staff in the change initiatives when you can.
7. Bring in new evidence to demonstrate that there are other ways of doing things that have been substantiated with research and are best practice.
8. Use brainstorming and nominal group processes to engage individuals in the solutions and generate ideas.
9. Always communicate as fully as you can. Information is power, and when you share information with the staff, they feel that you respect them enough to trust them with the information, which then engenders their trust in you.
10. Always put the customer at the center of all that the organization does. You can use the vision and mission statement to reiterate the alignment.
11. If things aren't going your way, be introspective and look first to your approach to see where the change is going wrong. Make those adjustments in your approach.

12. Lastly, be satisfied with baby steps. As long as you are moving forward with a change, you will get there. Twenty percent acceptance of a change is enough to move you to your goal over time.

Application to Practice

The metaphor of the phoenix is very applicable to the notion of change agency. The phoenix is a master of change and self-renewal. This is a straightforward application of theory to change your organization. Identify a change that you want to inculcate or evaluate a current change experience that has not been as effective as you would have hoped. Apply the theories in this chapter to the change, including the identification of a change theory, application of recommended steps and levels of thinking in innovation, and lastly, evaluate all the tenets of the culture. Develop a strategy for change or modify the strategy for failed change and apply. Continually evaluate the progress, introspect and make the modifications.

Chapter 8

Virtues, Attributes and Competencies of the Phoenix Leader

Just as treasures are uncovered from the earth, so virtue appears from good deeds, and wisdom appears from a pure and peaceful mind. To walk safely through the maze of human life, one needs the light of wisdom and the guidance of virtue.

Buddha

As we have discovered through the readings, leadership effectiveness is achieved through layers of concepts that weave together to create the ultimate leader. Three other concepts also come into play: virtues, attributes and competencies. The understanding of these concepts can help the emerging leader to continue to reflect on their success and hone effective leadership skills.

Virtues

Earlier we discussed the concept of values, which provide the fundamental basis of who we are. Values and virtues are oftentimes used interchangeably; however, they are two different concepts. To review, values are our core beliefs based on the influence of our parents, friends and experiences. Virtues are the next level, built on the foundation of values that manifest themselves as the character of an individual. Haden and Jenkins (2015) describe that leadership is the ability to make the right choices over and over again, and virtues provide the leader the framework that creates the ability to do that. They describe three different layers of virtues:

- *Cardinal virtues*: Courage, perseverance, wisdom and justice
- *Traditional virtues*: Hope, faith and charity
- *Relevance to today*: Humility, honesty and balance

Let's look at these virtues and apply them to leadership in an organizational setting. Although oftentimes virtues are associated with religion and faith, they can be generic and applied to other situations. The vision and mission of healthcare organizations rely on strong virtues that are dedicated to compassion, care and caring. These virtues will only be accepted and mirrored by the staff in the presence of a strong, virtuous leadership team.

Cardinal Virtues

Richert (2016) describes cardinal virtues as the most important of all virtues, secondary to the fact that all other virtues hinge on these four. From a linguistic perspective, the word *cardinal* is derived from the Latin word *cardo*, which means "hinge." The metaphor of the phoenix aligns nicely with these virtues since in order to reflect and reinvent yourself, these virtues are necessary.

Courage

Courage is defined as the strength to face something that frightens us. Whether we accept it or not, we all have fears. In Chapter 3 we spoke in depth about the ego and its contribution to fear. If we have strong egos, we can live in fear of our image and what others think of us. Over the years, I have seen many leaders that were willing to move forward with something that they knew was not going to work rather than admit the flaws in the beginning. Just recently I was in a situation whereby the leader actually fired her staff member and blamed them for a terrible outcome that was clearly her fault. She was new in her job and it was apparent that her ego overshadowed her notion of integrity. The result was that she had lost respect from all of us around her, and the relationship with her is now very strained. Rather than doing the right thing, she was willing to risk her image thinking that by deflecting and blaming others it would protect her in the long run, but it worked in the reverse. I have always seen these situations result in disaster for the leader over time when everyone figures out the truth. Courage is the ability to face adversity and do the right thing regardless of the outcome for you. Effective, proactive leaders should never get themselves into these situations.

Courage on the part of the effective leader is also related to the concepts of innovation and creativity, which we discussed in Chapter 7. Risk-taking is a necessary component of change, and with highly innovative solutions, the risk may be higher. Leaders that are going to be effective change agents need to be courageous.

Perseverance

When I think of perseverance, what comes to mind for me is the comedy movie *Galaxy Quest* with Tim Allen and Sigourney Weaver. Tim Allen played the part of Michael Nesmith, star of a hit sci-fi television series who is the commander on a spaceship. His mantra throughout the film is "Never give up, never surrender." The movie is actually very funny, and I continually use his mantra as it applies to many scenarios I have been in.

Leadership is not easy, and oftentimes it feels that we are continuously pushing this huge rock up a hill, facing tremendous resistance along the way. If a leader lacks perseverance, they will have a tendency to abandon their strategy for an easier path. There will be times when it is evident that certain approaches need to be abandoned, but that should be secondary to evidence that the strategy will not be successful and not simply from fatigue. I have mentioned several times that change takes time and it is important to apply the concept of "baby steps." As long as you are moving forward, you are moving, so keep it going. Eventually, the ball begins to roll downhill.

As leaders, we all have periods where we feel our work lives are disasters for a variety of reasons: terrible bosses, high-stress situations, financial pressures and outside pressures in our personal lives. I would be concerned if you did not have these experiences. I had an experience earlier in my career when my boss was called "Satan" by all around him. Needless to say, this was a tough environment to thrive in. Everyone was continually on edge, to the point that it was difficult for us to come to work on the days that we knew we had to interact with him. I experienced migraine headaches and an irritable bowel and kept catching colds secondary to the intense stress level. For seemingly no reason, in a large leadership meeting, he began yelling at me for something that I had not done. It was not uncommon for him to blow up at individuals in meetings, but it had never happened to me prior to this. I just told him that we could talk about this offline after I do some follow-up investigation, which made him even angrier. I kept myself emotionally pulled together for the rest of the day, but when I got home I fell apart and started crying because my ego was truly bruised. My husband was the one who had to listen to my litany of renderings until he asked, "What you are going to do about this?" That was the point when I realized that I had to face this. My husband also told me that he has always thought of me as the Tasmanian devil because when I get my teeth into something, I never let go and I never let it get me down. That metaphor for some reason translated to my personal strength. I would have preferred a reference from him like Joan of Arc or some respectful hero rather than a devil in a cartoon, but it was effective. The next day I went to Satan's office without an appointment, which was totally unacceptable. I walked in while he was on the phone, waited for him to finish and then told him that I did not appreciate his approach to me in the meeting and if we were going to have a relationship of mutual trust and respect, this could never happen again. What was interesting was the fact that he immediately apologized and stated that he did not realize his behaviors. Our relationship tremendously improved and he never treated me in that way again, although he continued to yell at others on the team. Moral of the story: Regardless of tough times, persevere and make sure that you are at least taking those baby steps.

Wisdom

> The saddest aspect of life right now is that science gathers knowledge faster than society gathers wisdom.
>
> **Isaac Asimov**

Knowledge is what we know, and wisdom is how we effectively apply it. New leaders can acquire a tremendous amount of knowledge from school, conferences, research and reading, but it takes experience to apply that knowledge and earn wisdom. In healthcare we value critical thinking as the way to approach healing and our industry, but critical thinking is the demonstration of wisdom over time in any work environment. The quest for wisdom is why we have residencies and internships and training for new employees to take the knowledge and apply it through the process of critical thinking.

Leaders can acquire wisdom by taking every experience, whether positive or negative, and reflect on the successes as well as what could have been done differently. The next challenge is to actually take the reflection to heart and make changes based on the learning. There is not a day that goes by where I don't learn something that I can apply to future scenarios. The key is to be aware of those opportunities and seize the learning. I like to use the terminology of pearls. During my seminars and training opportunities, I like to have a large sheet of paper and encourage people throughout the event to write pearls of wisdom on the paper for all to observe. What is a pearl for someone may be missed by someone else, so this approach helps with group learning and reflection.

Justice

There are many words available to define *justice*, but the ones that I feel relate the best to effective leadership are *impartiality* and *fairness*. I have heard many times from staff that they feel that they are not treated with fairness and that their manager treats other people differently. This could be secondary to the perception that others are preferentially getting the time off they want and they are not, or concerns as simple as my manager does not pay any attention to me. In this type of environment, the staff become fractured into different cliques, which leads to a reduction in teamwork and engagement. Remember that the perception of the staff is all that matters, even if you don't think their concerns are warranted. Their reality is their reality, and their reality is what needs to be dealt with.

The following suggestions are strategies that have consistently worked for me over time and have helped other leaders develop successful approaches:

1. First, it is important to realize that every staff member is important and valuable for what they bring to the team. We are not going to have the same affinity for everyone, and based on our core believes and values, we may feel more aligned with certain individuals that are more like us. This is normal and expected, but the key is to realize and appreciate the value that everyone brings.

2. Be deliberate when setting expectations of the staff, and then hold all the staff accountable to the same standards. If a leader does not set clear expectations, the staff have a tendency to work to their own standards, which will be different from person to person. Setting expectations up front levels the playing field for all and provides the framework

for performance excellence. Every organization will have behavioral expectations, but it is critical that the leader connect the dots for the staff and interpret the meaning of those policies. Remember, what you ignore, you endorse.

3. Maintain a high level of visibility and accessibility for all staff. It is not acceptable to make yourself available for some of the staff and not the others. Make sure that the staff realizes that they all have equal access to you so they cannot say that you are unfair.

4. Be diligent with recognition. It is important to develop recognition programs for the big accomplishments of the staff, but there will always be individuals that will not be involved in such big successes. Reward the usual. There are so many little things that your staff do on a day-to-day basis that could be acknowledged. The employee that goes up and beyond to accomplish something. The staff member that stays over to help for 4 hours. The employee that you observe consoling a family member or spending more time with a customer in a meaningful way. We feel that these are the things we do within the context of our jobs, but each one of these situations is an amazing giving of self. I make it a habit of mailing at least 20 thank-you cards a week to the staff to their homes, thanking them for those wonderful efforts. When I hear that someone did something from another leader, I ask them to email me their names and what they did so I can follow up on those as well. Gallup identified through their research that the number one way to engage staff is to simply be grateful for them.

Traditional Virtues

Traditional virtues hinge off the cardinal virtues and are those that are passed on traditionally from person to person, society to society, family to family and generation to generation. These include hope, faith and charity. These are strong within the religious community; however, I am going to discuss them in the context of leadership behaviors.

Faith

Most of us will associate faith with a strong belief in God; however, faith can also be defined as trust or confidence in someone or something. When I drive my car, I have confidence that when I slam on the brakes, the car will stop. In the work environment, I need to have faith in my leaders that they have my best interest at heart. Faith is the foundation of trust, which is vital to effective leadership. Remember again that trust is the hardest thing to earn but the easiest to lose.

Hope

Hope is the desire and expectation of something to happen and is very important to life as we know it. Viktor Frankl (2006) was an Austrian neurologist and psychiatrist that lived through the Holocaust. He outlined his amazing experiences in his book *Man's Search for Meaning* and described his ordeal in four of the worst concentration camps. Through this time, he watched his parents, his brother and his pregnant wife die, along with countless others. You would think that these awful experiences would destroy anyone, but Viktor Frankl developed his own way to survive. He found meaning in what was happening to him and in what he would do with his experiences. He began writing his book, which chronicled what was going on around him, on small pieces of paper or other materials that he found lying around the camp. He developed his philosophy of logotherapy, which is focused on finding meaning in the lives of his patients. What he observed throughout his experience was that he knew when people were going to die in captivity based on the change in their personal demeanor, followed by a total loss of hope for their futures. This was repeated over and over again. He survived his experience and went on to be a great professor, author and contributor to the science of psychiatry.

This concept of hope is important in organizations. The leader is the beacon of hope for their staff. To relay those feelings of hope to the staff, the leader needs to remain confident and positive. Even in tough times, when it appears that things could not get any worse, the staff needs to feel supported and conserve the feelings of hope.

Charity

When we think of the word *charity*, we have a tendency to think of it in the context of giving to others. Charitable giving is a great way to align staff around a good cause that helps them focus on others and not only their concerns. I have done a great deal of philanthropic work throughout my career, and I find that when I give, I receive so much in return. A leader can help their employees receive the gift of charity by encouraging them to become involved in the community or other initiatives for the needy. I have always expected my staff to create a legacy project that results in good for others. One of our teams built a house for Habitat for Humanity. This was an amazing project that took them 2 years to raise the funds for. All of us actually did the build together and took part in the dedication of the home to the needy family. Other projects included the organization of an after-school reading program for underserved children and Nurses 4 Detroit, a foundation that organized nurses from all over southeastern Michigan to help the community in various ways. Not only do these initiatives help others in meaningful ways, but they also are a tremendous way to build teamwork.

Charity is also the kindness we show toward one another and our tolerance in their differences. An effective leader can create a workplace based on charity toward each other whereby people give each other the benefit of the doubt when things are not going well, but also recognize and lift people up when they appreciate their actions and efforts. It is far easier to be engaged in this type of organization than an organization built on arrogance and what I call "one-upmanship."

Relevant Virtues

There are three virtues that are relevant to modern leadership (Haden and Jenkins, 2015): humility, honesty and balance. As I spoke of earlier in this book, one of the most important attributes of a leader is authenticity. The relevant virtues align nicely with the concepts of authenticity.

Humility

Merriam-Webster (2016e) defines *humility* as "a modest or low view of one's own importance; humbleness." Not to be confused with a low level of self-confidence. Conversely, the humble leader is extremely wise and so confident in their abilities that they don't need to be the center of attention.

I have had many situations in my career whereby I have been charged with projects and initiatives and my superiors took all the credit for my work, leaving me feeling like an invisible worker bee. I have observed this throughout my career, and the results on the staff can be devastating. In my observation, these leaders feel that if their staff look good, it makes them look bad. The reverse is actually true. When staff are lifted up for their work, they become more engaged and the rest of the staff notice the appreciation and also become more engaged. The leader actually is more recognized for the quality of their work. I recommend several actions that can be incorporated by the humble leader that will positively impact the staff.

■ Lose the *I* word. The leader does not become successful alone; it takes a team to achieve success.
■ Replace the *I* word with *us*. This approach brings people together and makes them feel part of the larger mission.
■ Lift up everyone. It is critically important to recognize others publicly for their work. Especially when working with other departments, this approach helps to build a solid relationship of respect between the silos.
■ Learn to say thank you, thank you, thank you. I send many thank-you cards a week to staff with personal, handwritten notes. These are sent to their homes. I have had countless staff come to me to say thank you for the thank-you card, and that I made their day. You also don't need to know the staff personally to recognize them in this way.
■ Listen to ideas. You are not the end all, be all of knowledge. Arrogant leaders need to get over themselves and realize that those at the point of service have the ideas. I have had some "wild" ideas from staff that when incorporated into the work environment were wildly successful. Staff are amazing thinkers if you eliminate their fear of contributing.
■ Use your staff's ideas. If you listen to ideas, you need to try some of those ideas. I was rounding on my units just recently and noticed that one of the floors in one of the rooms was blue and the others were beige. When I asked the staff why the one floor was blue, the staff told me that the past administrator, in the spirit of empowerment, asked them what color floors they would like when they refreshed the unit. The staff picked a neutral color. She did not like the color and started to replace the floors with ceil blue. It really looked horrible. The good news is that they stopped the refresh due to financial constraints, but the effects on the staff years later still remain. The staff said that they felt worthless and wondered why she asked them if she was going to drive her own agenda.
■ You have a lot to learn. Regardless of how long I have been in administration, every day I learn something valuable from my staff. As leaders, we do not have all the answers, but more importantly, we need to realize that we don't have all the answers and that there is always more value in learning.

Honesty

Honesty actually has two components in its definition, truthfulness and fairness. As leaders, there are many executive issues that are not appropriate to share with the staff and should not be shared with the staff. If there are changes that will affect the staff, however, if appropriate, they should be brought into the conversation. Mergers and acquisitions as well as reductions in staff present a delicate challenge for leaders in response to staff inclusion. In these cases, the entire leadership team needs to be aligned with appropriate talking points and strategies to reach out to the staff in a comprehensive manner. The best way to approach these issues is to communicate what you can and then be there to support the staff.

Also, during the course of regular leadership business, it is important to never lie to the staff or put yourself in a position where the staff may feel that you lied to them—as in the example of the floor color scenario I described in the last segment. It is also paramount that the commitment to honesty is applied to working with your colleagues and other departments. It will immediately ruin your credibility and limit the support that you will need from others to get your work done.

Balance

There are many ways to apply the concept of balance to leadership, from balancing schedules to competing priorities to financials. Because I truly believe in the importance of a strong personal "self" as the foundation for exemplary leadership, I will talk about balance in the context of personal balance. I personally do not really buy in to the concept of work–life balance, as I find that there is so much more to being balanced than just the connection to work and life. I like to use the term *work–life integration*. The reality is that high-level leaders, with the level of authority and responsibility that we have, can never run away from it. I am on call 24/7 and everyone has my cell phone number. I get called around the clock and texted because with technology, the invasion into our personal lives is easy and now a reality. As leaders, we need to feel compassionate and stay connected to our roles, so how do we make this integration work? I have ideas.

Let's first look at the perfect picture of what life balance looks like. Groysberg and Abrahams (2014) describe work–life balance as an elusive ideal and a complete myth. They talk about conquering some type of balance by making deliberate choices about which opportunities to pursue and which to decline. The inability to do this can lead to loss of relationships, family and personal focus. Their research, which included 4000 executives, suggested that those who were the most effective with managing their perception of work–life balance did the following actions:

- Defined personal success for themselves
- Managed technologies, that is, emails, cell phones, texts, and so on
- Built support networks
- Traveled selectively
- Relocated selectively
- Collaborated with their partners

They also found that both men and women felt that family tensions with work were more a woman's problem and not so much a focus for men. This was on both sides of the equation; the working women as well as the wives of the working husbands said the same. This is an astounding concept since healthcare has a very high percentage of women that will be affected by these conflicts. An even greater reason to pay attention to the issue. I also have been challenged with this as after finishing my diploma degree, I was pregnant with my son at the time I took my nursing boards. I took a very short leave and went back to work in 3 weeks. I then finished my BSN and went on to my MBA while I was pregnant with my daughter. I finished my doctoral degree several years later, all while working full-time and managing a family. I also was involved in other business endeavors concurrently, so I always felt this pressure. How did I manage it? I have a tendency to look at everything as a process and a plan. So, I analyzed my values and based my schedules around those.

Components of Balance

Let's break this down a bit and focus on the various components of balance since each one is inextricably linked to the other. If one area of your life is off balance, it affects the others.

With the reality of life, perfect balance is not a constant, but the awareness of how to manage those periods of stress and conflict can help. If you look back at your life you will identify many times of conflict, illness, problems with relationships, relocations, difficult children, problems at work and more that upset the balance of a personal life. We are never going to get away from these challenges but can make changes in other components to try to shift the balance back to midline. For instance, for me, when I am stressed I increase my workouts and sleep and I make those a priority until I get through the rough times. When my mom was very sick and dying, taking her to doctors, running her to the emergency department and visiting her in the hospital or nursing home placed tremendous pressure on me both emotionally and physically. Even with time pressures I would find time to at least march in place in front of the TV for a few minutes or stretch for a short period of time to clear my mind and decompress. These times in our life are also dangerous as they can lead to not so healthy ways to dealing with them, including drugs or excessive drinking. You need to find your healthy release. Here are what I find are the components of balance that are important to me, in order from the highest rank to the lowest.

Spirituality

Spirituality can be defined in the religious or nonreligious context. I am Catholic and do have a strong belief and practice of prayer that is foundational to me and my balance. I also see this in a broader context. My personal definition of spirituality is any meaningful activity that replenishes my soul. That could be my prayer, kayaking, love of nature or diversional activities, such as hobbies and charity work. Whatever means something to you is what will fill your spirit and make you feel whole. When you know what fills your spirit, you need to plan time for those activities.

Meditation

Meditation is a powerful tool to calm the mind and reset the thought process. I am not the most successful meditator, but I find that I don't need to be. Just taking time to be quiet and not think is calming and helps me reset my attitudes and thoughts. There are many ways to meditate and many courses available to help you meditate well. I make it simple for myself and take 10 minutes a day to sit quietly and try not to think. I imagine the sky as my canvas and when thoughts pop into my head, I just see them as clouds passing over and then quickly dismiss them. You can meditate at any time in the day that works for you. For me, this is vital to my balance.

Relationships

Groysberg and Abrahams (2014), through their research, identified one of the key issues with work–life balance as stress in personal relationships. I am far from a relationship expert and I don't claim to have any answers. What I have learned from my successful marriage of 43 years is that my husband has been integral to my support and a vital component of balance for me. I find that when things are not going well in other areas of my life, he props me up with his love and support. Regardless of whether you are married or in another type of relationship, in order to provide a contribution margin to your balance, the relationship has got to be supportive. My advice to friends and family has always been to be intolerant of relationships whereby you are not treated to the same level that you would treat yourself and to seek to repair or remove yourself from relationships that are toxic. At times that is easier said than done.

Lisa Petrilli (2016) recommends that it is important for the leader not only to find personal balance but also to support the staff in their quest for balance. She suggests that this can be done by first setting the example so that your staff know it is important to you. Other strategies include providing flexible schedules, stress reduction programs and opportunities for on-site relaxation and physical fitness activities.

Physical Activity

There are countless research studies on the importance of exercise to a healthy life. Hospital administration is a contact sport that requires stamina and energy. That stamina will only come from personally caring for yourself and increasing your physical activity. The following are the advantages of physical activity:

- Improves physical strength
- Strengthens the immune system
- Improves the cardiovascular system
- Improves the function of the digestive system
- Decreases fat
- Increases metabolism
- Improves flexibility
- Improves balance

- Increases endurance
- Restores personal control
- Decreases stress
- Improves self-esteem

There are many exercise options to choose from, and you will need to pick the best alternative for you. I always recommend that if you are new to exercise, seek the help of a personal trainer so that when you start your program you quickly see results. I was a personal trainer and aerobics instructor for many years, so I am familiar with the frustrations of not seeing results by not exercising appropriately. Always pick activities that you enjoy or you will not continue. My general recommendation is to just get moving. Increase your walking while you are at work. Get a step tracker and work your way up to 10,000 steps a day. Do some walking meetings and get a standing desk to build your core. Just get moving.

Nutrition

We always hear that you are what you eat, and there is plenty of evidence that this is true. Administrators have great opportunities for stress in their lives, and eating well can help mitigate the effects of stress. I have never been a fan of fad diets or trends. Decreasing fat and calories by staying away from processed foods while eating more natural foods is a simple and effective approach, especially if coupled with exercise.

Financial Stability

My last component of balance is that of financial stability. I do not mean this in the context of having a great deal of money or being perceived as "rich." I find richness in far more ways than just money. I see financial stability as being conservative with your spending. My trips to Haiti working with the kids in the mission and observing the community there showed me that I don't need as much as I thought I did to be happy. Spending within your means and keeping your debt down to manageable levels, investing and saving on a regular basis and building an emergency fund for unexpected costs are what most experts recommend (Figure 8.1). Figure 8.1 is my depiction of the hierarchical components of balance as I see them.

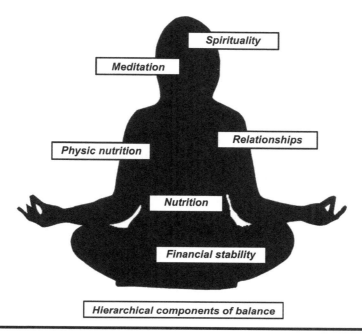

Figure 8.1   Components of balance.

Other Attributes of Successful Leaders

Before we leave this chapter, there are a few other attributes of effective leaders to explore that I think are critical. These include the concepts of fearlessness, power, assertiveness, inclusivity and consistency. Improving on these skills or adding these to your repertoire will help to round out your leadership toolkit.

Fearlessness

One of the things that I like most about my administrative roles is the fact that every day there was a new challenge, and oftentimes one that I did not feel I had the competency to address. This always raised some level of fear in my ability to address the issue. Over the years of my experience, I found that I actually had the inherent skills to address the issues even though I did not believe it at the time. Being fearless is vitally important because you as a leader are responsible for everything that comes your way. For instance, I have worked with many leaders that had the fear of confrontation. The result of this is that when the need to step into a situation arises, the first response is to ignore it and not engage. What you ignore, you promote, so this type of behavior reinforces to the staff that they can virtually do anything they want without the fear that the leader will engage and follow through on expectations.

The following are my thoughts on strategies to face your fears in the workplace:

1. *Do not react initially*: When faced with adversity, do not let fear grip you. Don't react to it immediately. I always recommend saying the second thing that comes to your mouth after you have thought rather than the first. Give yourself time for assessment of the situation so you have all the facts.
2. *Analyze the situation*: Review all the data and facts as they are presented to you and come up with your interpretation of what is being asked of you. Once you have data and facts, your assessment will be more accurate and comprehensive.
3. *Review your personal skillset*: Once you understand the situation, identify what attributes or skills you have that can be applied. If you identify that there are skills you need to achieve, then look for those who can help you with those components. You don't have to do it all and you don't need to know it all.
4. *Ask for clarification*: If there are areas of confusion in what is being asked of you, seek to clarify by asking the right questions. This will prevent any missteps due to misunderstanding and allow you to deliver a perfect product the first time.
5. *Ask for help*: It is not a weakness to ask for help from the experts. Seek advice or do your research on the topics you need and also those that interest you.
6. *Touch points*: Lastly, ask for touch-base points from your superior to make sure that you are moving in the right direction and are aligned with their thinking.

Fearless leaders are more successful with change. Taking risks in spite of personal fears is not easy, but it will help move your organization forward. Utilizing a comprehensive process to approach these fears is the answer to conquering them.

Powerful

Effective leaders are perceived to be powerful, so it is important to understand the concept of power and the positives and negatives that surround it.

There are many definitions of power, from physical strength to ability to conquer or get things done. In the context of leadership, the powerful leader has the capability of directing and influencing behaviors or events. The keyword is *influencing*. I see influencing as much different than causing change through force. The transformational phoenix leader will support those around them, make them feel comfortable with the change and help them successfully implement the change. Throughout history we have seen many examples of abuse of power, but utilizing this approach will not engender trust and improve engagement (Chand, 2014).

Types of Power

French and Raven (1960) studied the concept of power, and their theories have continued to be the foundation for the study of power today. They identified two major categories: positional and personal power. Positional power is that which is given inherent to the role. As an executive, you have certain powers inherent in your job description that are visible and understood by your subordinates. Conversely, personal power is the respect that you receive from others for your talent or your alliances with others in the organization. Within these two categories, they further identified subcategories under each heading. Their categories are as follows.

Positional Power

Legitimate

Job descriptions and organization charts provide the foundation for legitimate power. This is the power handed to you based on your role. It is also what is expected of you in your role. The level of position in the organization provides some advantage as to staff response; however, there still needs to be an effective approach to influence the staff to move the organization forward. I have worked for people that have made it a point to let everyone know that they are the boss and the organization responded based on fear, resulting in high turnover rates and low engagement scores.

Reward

Coupled with legitimate power is the ability to reward individuals for a job well done. This can come in the form of a raise, bonus or other methods of compensation. Reward can also come in the form of a simple "thank you," which is especially noticed by the staff if coming from their leader or especially individuals at the executive level. Along with the ability to give rewards is the power to take them away via demotions or elimination of benefits. This type of power is generally very well understood by the staff.

Coercive

This power is based on the individual's ability to punish staff for noncompliance or poor performance. This is an important type of power; however, it needs to be used effectively and only after the leader has set expectations. I have seen many leaders that have struggled with this. As I mentioned before, what you ignore, you endorse, even though it is not in compliance with the expectations of the organization. It has been my experience over and over that behaviors are ignored or tolerated until the leader reaches a breaking point, the straw that broke the camel's back, and now the staff member needs to be gone. If expectations are set and staff are coached with each breech of standard, coercive power can be effectively utilized and perceived as fair by the staff. In fact, leaders that effectively manage poor performers are more appreciated by their staff. Poor performers are a burden on their peers in many ways.

Informational

Informational power was not one of French and Raven's original five levels of power. It was added several years later when their research demonstrated that information is powerful and those with the information are perceived as more powerful because of it. I truly believe in transparency as a more effective approach to leadership. It is vital to share what can be shared and to not flaunt the information that you have and use this as leverage with others in the organization.

Personal Power

Expert

Regardless of whether you are a leader, your skills provide a great deal of power to those that need to employ those skills. If you have expert skills that can be utilized throughout the organization, this is a great opportunity for you to get more visibility in the organization and capitalize on those skills for promotions and recognition. Once recognized for this expertise, the organization will seek you out for your unique skill. You can leverage your talent if you make your skills known and offer to help on initiatives that could use your help or offer to be on committees to get you that visibility.

Referent

Referent power is a very interesting concept and fascinating to observe in the organizational setting. This power is perceived based on associations with higher-level individuals in the organization. In the C-suite, an example is the administrative assistants to the executives. These individuals have tremendous power in several forms; they are closely aligned with the executives, which provides them referent power, but they also have expert power in their knowledge of the organization, as well as their high-level skills in their role. By virtue of what they deal with, they have a very high level of "classified" information that makes them valuable to the organization. Other individuals that have referent power are those that may be or are perceived to be friends of the executives. There is the perception that these individuals have more information that has been received from the executive. It is important as a senior executive to be careful as to who is considered to be part of the senior leadership team. It is best to include those with the appropriate level of legitimate power and include other levels of leadership when it is appropriate to discuss certain issues.

Assertiveness

In order to effect change, the leader has to come across with a degree of assertiveness, meaning that they are confident and somewhat forceful in their approach. They need to get everyone's attention, sell a compelling story and have the strength and fortitude to follow it through. This approach, however, needs to be tempered so as not to tip the scales to aggressiveness, which is evidenced by a more hostile approach and at times perceived as on the violent side. If people feel that they are being bullied into a change, it will not happen and the leader will lose all respect. I worked with an individual in one of my past roles that was aggressive with anything that she wanted to do. She would embarrass and call out individuals and leaders in front of the senior executives and as a result had very little credibility in the organizations and a very difficult time achieving her goals. She continued to struggle throughout her tenure there and never understood why people did not respond positively to her. Yet it was clear to all around her.

Inclusivity

Effective leaders are inclusive. By this I mean that they have the ability to make everyone feel important. When included in decisions, whether it is at the point of service or in other larger projects, staff feel empowered and engaged. A savvy leader will include a diverse group of individuals since their thoughts and varying perspectives provide a wealth of new ideas. What I have seen in many scenarios is actually the opposite. Some leaders, especially those that do not like conflict, will have a tendency to put together homogenous groups with individuals that they perceive as like thinkers. We may also exclude individuals that we have had conflict with in the past. It is actually productive to include such individuals because they have a tendency to be critical and bring up conflicting issues for discussion.

Consistency

I have spoken about the need for consistency early in the book, but I wanted to highlight the importance of consistency as a competency for effective leaders. For the most part, healthcare as an industry is chaotic. Continual changes have a tendency to keep the staff in a state of flux and unrest. One of the most important things a leader can do is maintain a consistency in approach that increases trust on the part of the staff. Here are some recommendations to maintain consistency in your approach to leadership.

- Personal issues and conflicts should never be taken into the work environment.
- If there is any unrest or conflict in your work relationships, the staff should never know it.
- Always verbally and physically (body language) support your leaders.
- Always verbally and physically (body language) support your organization and the decisions of senior leadership.
- Always look at the positives of a situation and emphasize the good.
- Maintain a high level of visibility with the staff.

Personal SWOT analysis

Strengths	Weaknesses	Opportunities	Threats

Figure 8.2   Personal SWOT analysis.

- Always react with the same controlled demeanor.
- Never lose faith in the power of you or your staff. They are what make magic happen.

Application to Practice

In this chapter, we focused on several virtues and competencies of effective leadership that expanded on some of these concepts. Successful leaders continually learn and work to improve themselves. This ability to change and adapt is the foundation of a phoenix. To apply this to practice, take a little time to review your behavior in the context of virtues and competencies. The best way to accomplish this is to conduct a personal SWOT analysis that is focused on this topic. Figure 8.2 has a template for a SWOT analysis that you can use.

Chapter 9

Foundational Behaviors of the Phoenix Leader

Leadership is much more an art, a belief, a condition of the heart, than a set of things to do. The visible signs of artful leadership are expressed, ultimately, in its practice.

Max Depree

Throughout this book, we have covered many strategies and behaviors for successful leadership. In this chapter, we focus on some very important behaviors coupled with strategies to include them in your leadership development plan. These behaviors include visibility and accessibility, role modeling, proactivity versus reactivity, utilization of data and aligning of vision and mission.

Visibility and Accessibility

Early in my doctoral program, I read the book *Lincoln on Leadership* (Phillips, 1992), which spoke to Abraham Lincoln's effective strategy of being visible to his troops. It described how he traveled for days into the field to spend time with his soldiers, to show them he cared about them and was there for support. He was also willing to partake in the same activities they did and to do himself whatever he expected them to do. Truly an amazing role model.

If you think about the period of time in which Lincoln led his army, this approach to visibility was a tremendous commitment and probably extremely challenging at that time. Despite the challenges, he made the effort to be there with his team and to do himself what he asked his team to do. Given this current era of email, technology, FaceTime, videoconferencing and modern smartphones, there is no excuse for staff to not have accessibility and visibility with their leader, yet I frequently observe leaders that seem more invisible because of this technology. They choose to use only the technology in lieu of face time with their staff. It is not the same thing as being there.

I cannot tell you how many times I have worked with organizations and have asked the staff about their leaders. Oftentimes, they respond with the answer that they don't even know what they look like and they never see them in their departments. It is impossible to lead the organization if the staff does not even know who their leaders are. It is critical to develop a comprehensive plan to establish and maintain visibility and accessibility. Here is what works for me:

■ Maintain an open-door policy and let the staff know about it. The only concern with an open-door policy is that it cannot be used to complain about their superiors. This ignores the chain of command. If there are concerns with their leaders, they need to be coached to approach them first before you intercede.

■ Be visible in the work areas. It is not just about walking through and saying hi. My recommendation is that you actually schedule time to work the units or departments to learn about their unique concerns and challenges. I make it a practice to work in one area every week for 3–4 hours just to be close to my staff. My administrative assistant considers that protected time unless there is an emergency that needs to be dealt with. While on the floor, I actually work with a staff member while I am there. I also take time to ask the staff to let me know how they would like to improve their work environment and how I can help. With this approach, people are very positive and willing to share. Also, wearing scrubs rather than a suit visually sends the statement that you are one of their team.

■ Develop other strategies for face time with employees, including focus group meetings and town halls. I find that focus group meetings with small groups (three or four people) helps to create a safe environment where employees feel comfortable to share. With large groups, the extroverts are usually the individuals that talk, oftentimes shutting down the introverts. Their opinions are just as valuable and should be heard. Town halls are also great opportunities to bring larger groups together to provide information that is pertinent to the organization. These should be done around the clock to reach all the staff.

■ Use technology such as email, blogs and videoconferencing. These are especially effective if work units are not local.
■ Create a robust website that profiles the organization and highlights the staff.

Create Visibility for Your Staff

Platske (2016) suggests that an effective leader also focuses on the visibility of their staff to the organization as well as visibility for themselves. She suggests seven steps:

1. Have a visible written plan
2. Know thy personality
3. Create power partnerships
4. Presence
5. Set your priorities
6. Chart the progress
7. Invest in professional and personal development

It does make sense to me that allowing the staff to receive visibility will lead to recognition for them, and that would help to increase engagement. It is always an advantage to work on personal visibility in ethical and professional ways. We will talk about that later when we cover personal branding.

Role Modeling

We must acknowledge … that the most important, indeed the only thing we have to offer our students is ourselves. Everything else they can read in a book.

D.C. Tosteson

I really enjoyed reading this quote by Tosteson. I have committed myself to lifelong learning, but as leaders, we need to realize that part of our role is to enable our staffs to also be lifelong learners. Especially in the challenging times of modern industry, technology and approaches to products, services and the expectation of the consumer are continually changing, requiring the staff to keep up with this new knowledge and pace of action. Effective role models can inspire this level of learning. I still remember today my professors and teachers that helped me make those twists and turns in my life through their role modeling and resulting inspiration. These individuals truly fit the definition of a role model as someone that others like and want to emanate.

Cruess and Cruess (2008) published key points that highlight effective role modeling and its value in organizations; however, these points can generally be applied to the value of role modeling in the greater context. It is valuable to know about the advantages of role modeling to effectively utilize it. I truly believe that effective leaders are successful role models that people identify with and attempt to mirror their behaviors.

Advantages of Role Modeling

There are many advantages and disadvantages of role modeling that need to be considered. Role modeling needs to be done effectively by positive role models and not negative ones. It is not uncommon to have new staff start and be paired with preceptors or staff that are negative. This role modeling has a tendency to impart a negative spin on the new person and, at times, poor practices. What we do know is that role modeling is a powerful tool for teaching and mentoring as long as it is done in a positive way with the appropriate mentors.

When we teach, we learn. That is one of the great advantages I enjoyed while teaching classes. It kept me current and on the edge of research. An advantage of role modeling is that is helps to improve performance by providing learning opportunities for the mentors as well as the mentees.

Role modeling is a privilege as it allows us as mentors to have an impact on the future of healthcare as we help to grow the next level of healthcare providers. Cruess and Cruess (2008) describe that we model activities both consciously and unconsciously to those surrounding us. This makes it imperative that we are cognizant of our behavior and always making sure that we are presenting a professional demeanor. The other important concern to realize from the Cruess body of work is that role models actually contribute to character development of the staff. This is a tremendous responsibility.

Proactivity versus Reactivity

I feel that one way to describe our current environment is that it is chaos theory at its finest. However, if you look at trends in the data, even amid chaos, there is a repeatability phenomenon over time. Regardless, in my observation, we have a tendency to be more reactive rather than proactive. A savvy leader will first know the trends and follow the data, but more importantly, will react in a proactive way. Staffing variabilities is a great scenario to present. We know when we need increases in staffing, but oftentimes due to financial constraints we don't add staff or adjust the schedules appropriately for these variations. There are many approaches to scheduling to adopt if the leader is proactive and utilizes the data appropriately.

Another way for leaders to remain proactive is to continually evaluate the environment surrounding the organization with regard to changing demographics, new technology and competition. Leaders need to read these clues and execute strategies based on the intelligence. In my experience, one of my organizations moved our obstetrics department to one of the suburban hospitals secondary to the aging of the population, resulting in reduced volumes. The growth was in the suburbs with a younger population, so the move was made. These at times are difficult decisions to be made, however important to the financial solvency of any organization.

Use of Data

I am old enough (did I really say that?) to remember a time in my industry where the focus was primarily on finance, with little to no focus on outcomes. With the recognition of the work of Edward Deming, manufacturing led the way to quality and efficiency by focusing on zero defects. This approach began to reach other industries far before hospitals began to utilize data and realize that they had the responsibility to improve outcomes. As new processes for analytics began to arise, as well as demands by the government to look at healthcare in different ways, organizations began to attempt to analyze data that focused on outcomes and other issues. The result has been that organizations became data rich yet information poor. I still think that is a problem today. Wang and Hajli (2017) identified tremendous value to organizations through the development of analytical capabilities. They define big data as the ability to manage enormous amounts of data but, more importantly, to distill and transform this data to a usable focus for the leaders to react to it. They also described the need to encompass "speed to insight," which in my experience seems lacking at times. Is it that healthcare organizations are inherently slow to respond? Or are healthcare organizations still unsophisticated in the utilization of data? Wang et al. (2015) describe the notion of applying the data to dynamic capabilities, which is where organizations seem to struggle. Here are my approaches to develop an organization's skill, which leads to learning and improvements in outcomes, quality, safety and efficiency.

Do Not Fear Big Data

All leaders have varying, inherent capabilities and comfort levels with certain skills, and it is not uncommon to be leery of data. We are all wired differently. I have had many leaders over the years tell me, "I just don't like the IT stuff." First, there is a difference between IT and the utilization of data. Leaders should all adopt the desire for this learning since this is truly the only way we stay current and retain the capability to make enlightened change. Data is simply a component of that. As with any opportunity, it is important to find ways to improve the competency, whether that be utilizing experts in the organization, reading, doing course work or reviewing what you already know. Eliminating this fear, if you have it, is the first step to moving forward.

Study All Problems and Deficiencies

The use of data is unbounded and can be applied to any scenario. I have applied data to small projects focused on one work area, as well as large sweeping organizational change. Data not only confirms your beliefs in the deficits of the process but also improves your credibility through verification. The application of data after an intervention keeps you focused and on track and improves the likelihood for success.

Share the Data Widely

Over my years working with leaders, I have heard quite frequently that some of them refuse to share data widely because they feel that it is sharing their dirty laundry and that they will not be looked upon favorably by their leaders. I believe that full transparency and sharing this data, and then fixing it, is more valuable to the success of the leader. Also, sharing the data engages the staff in the problem and has the potential for reaching out for help to other departments or experts in the organization. I am never afraid of "poor" results because they provide so much opportunity for improvement. But then you need to improve.

Plan Interventions around the Data

Build your intervention around the data. Identify the deficiencies found in the data and then establish your goals and timeframes. Within the plan, focus all the touch-base events around review of the data elements and sharing of the information.

Build a Comprehensive Approach

Data is an integral component of process improvement regardless of the model you use in your organization. What I find in organizations is that more often than not, we try to utilize best practices or ideas before we look at the data. For instance, utilizing a healthcare example, in the effort to improve falls, we instituted the appropriate strategies and focused on things like obstacles in the room that caused the fall with little results. When we went back to take a "fresh look" at our approach, we expanded our analysis to include physiological components of falls and found that we had opportunities with the choice of sedatives, pain medications and sleepers. This was interesting to our physicians, who immediately began to make changes in these practices. We also found that the age of patients that were falling was actually much younger than those we thought were candidates for falling. In working with these younger patients, they told us that they needed to feel independent so they wanted to do things for themselves that oftentimes resulted in falls. There was a whole host of aha moments for us that totally changed our paradigm of falls and our resultant response to them.

Use Special-Cause Variation in Your Analysis

This is just an interesting observation for me, but I have frequently seen that when a problem rises to the surface (even though it has been a problem for a while), leaders overreact and feel the need to fix it now. The reaction is one of fury to put things into place, so the tendency is to throw everything up against the wall and hope something sticks. If the numbers improve with this approach, the problem is that we don't really know what intervention was the cause of the improvement. The more effective approach is to identify the interventions, incorporate them into a rollout plan and then institute them one by one over time. The data should be analyzed utilizing special-cause variation to see what intervention actually resulted in the improvement, and then to hardwire those that actually cause a positive effect. As an example, in one of my emergency departments, in the effort to improve patient satisfaction, we hired comfort care staff to address patient needs. We saw no improvement with this intervention, yet we spent a great deal of money on the project. We analyzed the satisfaction data and met with patients to find out that their real concern was being informed. When we changed some scripting for the staff and explained how important this was to the patients, we started to see improvements in our scores as identified by special-cause variation.

I find that there are best practices that should be considered for use; however, every organization is different, so the initiatives need to be customized to fit the nuances of a particular organization and the industry that its resides in.

Develop Data-Sophisticated Leaders

One leader cannot do everything alone, but it is also true that one leader cannot effectively analyze and manage all problems personally across the organization. To improve the reach of the leader, all leaders in the organization need to have a good grasp of data and quality improvement. It has always been my practice to have all my managers and directors obtain at least yellow belts in Six Sigma certification, along with Kaizen expertise. There also needs to be access to black belts across the organization for support when necessary.

Develop Data-Sophisticated Staff

Lastly, it is important to improve the sophistication of the staff in relation to the understanding of, and response to, data. This can be accomplished by making sure that the staff sees all the data that relates to their units, along with the goals for improvement. Data should be presented at all staff meetings, town halls and council meetings. Graphs should also be available to review on communication or huddle boards depending on your organization's approach.

Creating this comprehensive and sophisticated learning organization takes time. As I have said repeatedly in this book, the flavor of the sundae starts at the top, so if the leaders are focused on data, over time, it will become the fabric of the work and a consistent approach to problems. It is also exciting and motivating for the staff to see improvements to validate that they are making a difference.

Communication of Vision and Mission

All the aspirations of a leader will go by the wayside without the ability to align the organization. This is most effectively done by communicating salient vision and mission statements. My simplified definition of vision is "what we want to be when we grow up," and the mission statement is "how we are going to get there." We will discuss the more scientific definitions of both, but I find that breaking things down to more pedestrian language makes sense to all.

Vision Defined

Vision is a futuristic concept focused on what the organization aspires to be. If communicated effectively across the organization, this can be very exciting to the staff. Everyone wants to be part of a winning team, and effectively crafting and framing the vision can ignite the staff and improve engagement. For the most part, the vision should not change and is a result of the culture created by the founders and modified by the current leadership. Strategies to achieve the vision may change over time based on changes in the environment, but the foundational components will not. Vision along with mission should be the centerpiece of all communication and a strong component of the brand.

Mission Defined

Conversely to vision, mission articulates the purpose of the organization and why it exists. The mission statement will guide most of the decisions on the direction of the organization. For instance, if part of the mission statement includes a commitment to academics, decisions made in the organization will be evaluated in the context of whether they fulfill the mission of education. If research is in the mission statement, decisions on new programs and technology will need to be aligned with the opportunities that these new endeavors provide for research. Safety, quality and service are also strong elements of the mission in most healthcare organizations. The mission statement also provides the foundation for strategic planning in the creation of strategies to move the organization to its goals.

Just as important to align the staff with vision is to make sure the staff understands the mission of the organization. The mission statement should be part of all onboarding and orientation, a foundation for expectations and behaviors and strongly supported by all leaders.

Modern Approaches to Vision and Mission Statements

Traditional mission and vision statements have been around for decades. What is important is that whatever the mission and vision statements are, they clearly represent the organization and give employees something to rally around. To improve the rally potential, some organizations are moving away from traditional vision and mission statements to formats that are more action focused and easy to understand. The term *vision* is being replaced with *ambition* to translate the message more succinctly to the staff that the organization is ambitious and clearly moving forward.

Upholding the vision and mission is usually a pillar of some sort—individual areas of focus that will help the organization be successful. Titles such as *finance, people, quality* and *safety* are some common themes utilized. In some organizations, the pillars are being replaced by strategic imperatives that tell a greater story of how the organization will achieve its goals. An example could be *affordability* instead of *finance*, which is geared toward supporting the customer by understanding their financial burdens.

Lastly, corporate values that have been represented by a set of words, such as *integrity* and *loyalty*, are being replaced by action statements that also tell more of a story in the hope that they will guide behavior. An example would be, "We never settle for second best" or "We all support each other." Whatever format you choose, the underlying goal is to unite the organization to establish unified movement toward the achievement of the mission, ultimately resulting in financial success.

Aligning the Organization

As with any leadership success, the alignment of the organization is key to its success. Without staff buy-in, the chance of success is grim. Remember, it is those at the point of service that will ultimately be responsible for executing the strategies, and they need to believe in them. The lack of alignment of the staff is solely the responsibility of the leader; they need to develop strategies to achieve alignment of all staff. Most of the reasons for lack of staff buy-in surround the lack of knowledge on the part of the staff. As I mentioned before, communication is a great illusion in many organizations. We also need to remember that communication needs to include all generations, diverse populations, various learning styles and 24/7 schedules, where the midnight shifts usually have less exposure to leaders. Here are some suggestions:

- Create succinct vision and mission statements that all can understand and be able to repeat (they should fit on a tee shirt).
- Make the vision and mission part of the organizational brand.
- Make the vision and mission statements visible throughout the organization on banners, signs and other sources of media and material.
- Make the vision and mission statements part of all onboarding processes for new staff.
- Make the vision and mission statements visible for all training for current staff.
- Expand the vision and mission statements to include the various pillars that the organization will use to achieve the vision and mission.
- Have the mission visible on all documents, such as minutes from meetings and strategic plans.
- Start all large and corporate meetings with a review of the mission and vision statements.
- With any conflicts or adversity, bring the team back together by focusing efforts toward the vision and mission.
- Make sure that all leaders are aligned and moving in the same direction; it is important to remove those that will not become part of the journey.

If the leader puts the vision and mission at the center of all they do and try to implement, it is like "mom and apple pie." Using the vision and mission in this way can unify the entire organization and help to engage the staff. Once this foundation is set, strategy can move forward with less barriers.

Application to Practice

Several topics in this chapter relate to aligning the organization through various strategies. The first step to the application of these processes is to evaluate how well your organization is performing. Ask yourself the following questions with regard to the various topics around visibility and accessibility.

Visibility and Accessibility and Role Modeling

- Am I as visible to the staff as I should be?
- Do I know my staff? Names, roles and personal facts?
- Do I understand their work?
- If someone asked my staff who their leader was, would they say yes or no, never see them?
- Am I an effective role model to my staff?
- Do I walk the talk?
- Is my leadership team visible?
- Do they know their staff by name?
- If I asked them if they know their leaders, would they say yes or no, never see them?
- Are my leaders effective role models?
- Do they walk the talk?

Use of Data and Proactive Approaches

- Am I and my leaders comfortable with the utilization of data and application to process improvement?
- Do I take a proactive approach versus reactive approach to problem solving?
- Are my leaders familiar with the metrics that they need to focus on and how to apply them to improving practice?
- Is my staff familiar with the metrics that affect them and their practice?

Communication of Vision and Mission

- Am I aligned with the vision and mission of the organization I am in?
- Are all my leaders aligned with the vision and mission of the organization?
- Do all my staff know and support the vision and mission of the organization?

The answers to these questions can provide great insights into how effective you and your leaders are with these concepts. Alignment of the staff is critical to any leader's success, so in your findings, strategies should be developed around any variances or weaknesses you identify. Then as a phoenix leader, evolve in these areas and enjoy the successes as a result.

Chapter 10

Becoming a Phoenix Leader

I don't care who you were. I care who you are and I am more concerned with who you are going to become.

Baylor Barbee

We covered a great deal of information up until this point, and now the plan is to pull these concepts together to begin your strategy for personal growth as a leader. The focus will be on several concepts not yet covered but very important to your success, followed by a strategy and template for you to follow. It is time for your transcendence.

Self-Reflection

Self-reflection has been defined as the art of being with yourself. I think the choice of the word *with* is powerful in that it suggests an alignment with your being. Armknecht-Miller (2014) describes self-reflection as the leader's opportunity to look into themselves and identify potential areas for personal growth as well as problematic traits, and develop strategies to overcome these issues. She further describes that leaders who do not reflect perceive themselves as perfect and therefore close themselves to personal evolution. This arrogance cheats the leader out of great potential but also cheats the staff by stifling their learning as well. We spoke at length about the notion of ego, which is the reason that some leaders will have difficulty with self-reflection.

How to Self-Reflect

There are all types of methods for self-reflection, some very complicated and comprehensive. As a very busy leader, I need to approach such strategies with a simpler approach. Simply taking time to think. When I am confused or frustrated, I give myself time to think. My staff even know when I need time to think and will say, "Is it time to think?" This is different from the practice of meditation since it is focused on particular topics. I start by taking time to be quiet and review the situation or the day. I find it helpful to ask myself the following questions:

- What went well today?
- What did not go well today?
- What did I learn from the day?
- What could I have done differently?
- What is my overarching goal for learning tomorrow?

Figure 10.1 shows the template that I use. I don't necessarily do this daily, but I find that it is incredibly valuable when I am not happy with my performance with something that did not go well in either my personal or professional life. I do the best to try to observe the answers rather than criticizing them, which begins to create clouds of doubt. I also focus on the positive first and the learning second. This is a vital discipline for me, and I find that it helps me be better. Just as it is important for the leader to learn the art of self-reflection, it is also important to teach this skill to your leadership team and staff. This can help build the foundation for an enlightened organization.

Gratitude

There are three components of gratitude: being thankful, showing appreciation and returning kindness. All three of these align nicely together to demonstrate that those who are grateful for what they have and give back through kindness feel better about themselves and are honored in the organization. My greatest awakening to the notion of gratitude was when I started to help author Mitch Albom with his orphanage in Haiti. Mitch and I worked on several of his charities in Detroit together, but he asked me to help him with an orphanage he acquired shortly after the earthquake of 2010. What he needed from me was to medically evaluate the kids who were very undernourished and not well cared for.

My daily reflections

Date:_____

What went well today?

What did not go well today?

What did I learn from the day?

What could I have done differently?

What is my overarching goal for learning tomorrow?

Figure 10.1   Reflection template.

The first time I went to Haiti with Mitch, I took a team of medical professionals with me to help with the physical evaluation of the kids and the
development of a health improvement strategy. What I found there was truly
life changing and reframed my mind as to how grateful I should be for what
I have. The kids were eating rice and beans every day at 7:00 a.m. and 7:00
p.m., with no snacks throughout the day and drinking only water. They
were allowed to have chicken on Christmas. Because of their poor diet, they

were far below the American growth chart for children. We changed their diet, included protein on a daily basis and added a lunch and snack, and in 1 year they were all on the growth chart and very healthy. We made sure that they were immunized and built them beds and a school and provided other enrichment activities, like art and music. It was so much fun to watch them eat their first peanut butter and jelly sandwiches.

I would cry all the way back from Haiti on the plane. I could not believe that parents gave their kids away or abandoned them because they could not take care of them. From that moment on, material things were not important to me. I became so grateful for what I had and now begin every day being grateful for simply waking up. Once I wake up, everything from that moment on is an opportunity and a gift. I am grateful every day for Mitch and the opportunity he provided to me to make me a better person. Hard work, heat, dirt, bugs, malaria, cholera and the violence that I experienced in Haiti were so worth the love and gratitude from the kids. In fact, my last book was dedicated to Chika, one of our little girls who died of a terrible brain tumor.

Louise Hay (1996) is one of the most prolific writers in the areas of gratitude. She believes that gratitude is linked to everything we do, from our health to life successes. She has many strategies for personal reflection and the evolution to a life of gratitude.

Continuous Evaluation of Goals, Strategies and Approaches

Over the years, I have observed many leaders going to great lengths to establish goals and develop strategies only to put them on the shelf. If the intent is to develop these pieces of work and then put them on a shelf, why bother? These plans need to be living documents that you refer to on a regular basis and react to the progress or lack thereof. The environment is continuously changing, so your approaches to issues and goals may change as well.

Lifelong Learning

I have mentioned several times through this book the importance of lifelong learning, but it is important to realize the approaches to lifelong learning. There are many ways to incorporate lifelong learning into our lives, both formally and informally.

Formal Approaches

Formal approaches are those that we search out to learn what we feel we need to learn. These include furthering education through degree programs, conferences, reading, webinars, ongoing competency programs through work and certifications.

Informal Approaches

Even more valuable than formal learning is the informal opportunities that we oftentimes don't even realize are learning opportunities. These can be personal experiences that we have that provide insight. We spoke of reflection as a way to learn. Another important way to learn is through observation. I am always open to learning through observation in meetings, watching behaviors and responses between individuals and canvassing the environment. I not only focus on those that I honor and try to emulate but also learn from individuals that are not professional and poorly interact or don't support the organization. This gives me a look into how I should not behave.

Mentors

Mentors are critical to the growth of any leader. They support us and are willing to teach in a way that grows us through their giving. I have had and still cherish many of my mentors, who today remain great friends and people that I feel I can reach back to for help. They have become part of my valuable network, and I have many contacts that I may need in the future. My recommendations for the selection of mentors include the following considerations:

- Reach out to mentors that will bring you a skill that you don't have or contacts that you need.
- Feel free to reach out to those individuals who you think would never help you. You will be surprised at those who are willing to help.
- Select older mentors to help you with a perspective of wisdom from the past.
- Select younger mentors to help you visualize the future. Younger mentors can help keep you fresh and thinking about the future.
- Don't ever feel that you are a burden to mentors. They know that they have growth opportunities as well. I love mentoring and always feel that I learn as much from those whom I mentor as they learn from me.

Develop an Effective Personal Brand

If I asked you what your personal brand is, you may answer that you don't have one. Regardless of whether you realize your brand, you have one. A brand is simply a promise to others based on an experience that they have with you. It is what people say about you when you are not in the room. Let us explore this concept a bit closer by looking at some famous brands.

It is 100° outside and you are tired and thirsty. You decide to get something to drink, so you go to your fridge and get a can of Coca-Cola and a glass of ice. Your mouth starts to water and as you pop the lid off the can, you immediately hear the fizz and experience the delicious smell. As you pour your coke over your ice, you see the bubbles and the rich caramel color. When you take that first sip, the cold wetness and flavor overwhelm your senses as your thirst begins to become a distant memory. In other words, it is not Coca-Cola that is the centerpiece of the brand, but rather the experience you have while drinking it. If you don't like coke, feel free to substitute your favorite drink in the context of the experience. You can think of many powerful brands and what their promise is to their consumers.

Your personal brand is what people experience when they are around you. Are you someone who helps others? Are you a chronic complainer? Do you volunteer for committee work and projects or do you just get by? People around you are observing you all the time and are crafting impressions of you that become your personal brand even though you don't realize it. Here are a couple of things to remember when thinking about your personal brand:

■ Everything that you say and do affects your personal brand.
■ Once lost, a personal brand is hard to recover.
■ Your personal brand encompasses all your behaviors, appearance and relationships.
■ Your personal brand is all about how you make people feel through their experiences with you.

Because your personal brand is so important to your organizational success, it is vital that you take control of your brand and actually craft a vision for yourself and your brand, one that you want people to recognize and remember.

Benefits to Personal Branding

The stronger the personal brand, the more valuable you are. When you become valuable, you can demand a premium. Look at Starbucks. Who would have thought many years ago that people would spend more than $1 for a cup of coffee? The Starbucks brand is so strong that they are getting far more than $1 for their coffee. It is the strength of the brand that commands a premium. You can be the premium.

Other benefits of a strong personal brand include your differentiation from others in the organization, which increases your visibility. This allows you to continue to build on your expertise and improve your self-confidence, and helps you achieve your goals. Because you are so valuable to the organization, opportunities will come your way and you can pick and choose what you would like to work on.

Secrets to Developing a Successful Brand

Creating your personal brand is fun. Here are some steps to follow.

Give yourself a title: Think of what your strengths are, led by your passion, and develop a clear vision for who you want to be and how you want to be remembered. For me, my passion is leadership, so I chose the personal brand title "Dr. Val, Leading Leaders." This brand is copyrighted, and I use it on all my documents, cards, mailings and presentations.

Create a strong offering to others: When you identify your strengths, see how those strengths can help others. In one of the classes I was teaching, one of my DNP students called himself the "tool leader" because he was into tools and had a passion for building things in his personal life. He applied that discipline of planning and construction to his approach to building systems as a leader. He felt that some of his strengths with this competency would be planning, creativity and the development of solid products and services. What do you have to offer?

Be a personality to remember: Do not be afraid to be bigger than life. I don't mean that you need to be obnoxious. I mean to be authentic, as we described, and engaging and open to any opportunities that come your way. Be humble, but make sure that people know your skillset and your willingness to be part of something bigger.

Presentation, presentation, presentation: I mean this in two different ways. Always present yourself as a complete professional, and by that I mean demeanor and dress. If you wear skinny pants, short skirts or clothes that look like you just jumped off a boat, you will not be taken seriously. If your company does casual Fridays, wear those at that time, but during business hours, present yourself as a consummate executive. I have always been told to dress for the role you want and not the role you have. As a manager, I was wearing suits unless I was in scrubs working with my staff. I remember interviewing candidates for an executive director position in my organization. One of our internal candidates that applied showed up to the interview wearing revealing, casual clothing. I immediately did not see an executive and felt that this individual would not represent the department well. After the position was filled, I told her that she was not the choice, but I also told her why so she would learn from this experience. We all would like to think that we are nonjudgmental, but the reality is that we subconsciously judge everyone based on our past experience, and that is what sets the first impression, which is everything in some scenarios.

The second component to this is public presentations. If you have a fear of public speaking, take steps to get over it. I always recommend that you present to small groups and work your way up to larger groups. The largest group that I presented to was 8000 people in a huge conference center. I don't suggest that you start there, but public speaking is just like anything else you do. The more experience you get, the better you become. There are also speaking coaches available to work with you to hone those skills. As an executive, you will need to present to very important audiences and deliver your message succinctly and expertly.

Deliver What You Promise but Don't Promise What You Can't Deliver

The worst thing to do is overpromise. Once you make a promise and fail at the delivery, you allow your audience to doubt your capabilities. It is better to overdeliver and underpromise. You will need to assess what is asked of you in order to understand your response.

Ingredients of an Effective Personal Brand

Many authors cite ingredients of an effective personal brand, but I sum them up into a simple five-step equation (E5), which stands for

- Energy: Never giving up and continuously moving forward
- Energize: The ability to mobilize people

- Edge: Staying on the edge and leading forward with courage
- Execution: Getting things done
- Exemplary practice: Excellent delivery utilizing the best practice and research

Most of all, in relation to your personal brand, have fun, be creative and enjoy the evolution.

Application to Practice

Wow! We have covered a great deal of information throughout this entire experience, and I hope I have imparted some valuable wisdom to you all. The last step in the dance is to take all this information and put it into a personal leadership development plan. I am including the template that I use, which is simple yet comprehensive. Remember that I believe that leaders have enough on their plate that self-development, although vital to personal growth, should be straightforward and easy to achieve (Figure 10.2).

Figure 10.2   Personal goal development.

	Personal leadership strategic plan			
Goal:_____				
Objective	**Tactics**	**Target date**	**Comments**	

Figure 10.3 Personal strategic plan.

Here are the steps to develop your comprehensive leadership development plan. The first step is to identify your goals. You have done your SWOT analysis and have some direction for evaluating areas that you are interested in working on. I have created this template with five goal statements, but you could begin working on three and then expand. The goal statements should be very defined with what you want to achieve; that is, a goal statement could be "develop my personal brand" or "improve my presentation skills" or "improve my finance skills." Anything that you want to do, there are no limits. The second step is to evaluate your strategy around the achievement of these goals. Figure 10.3 shows my document to help you stay on track with your strategy, although you can use any methodology that you wish. The ultimate goal is to get you where you want to be, not how you get there.

Conclusion

It has truly been an honor to share with you anything that has worked well for me in my career. I hope that this wisdom can help you to move your leadership career forward without making some of the same mistakes that I have. Although learning through trial and error is ultimately effective, paying attention to the literature and those people who have been there done that may help you avoid some of the land mines of leadership. I have enjoyed being your personal coach through this journey, and I wish you the best of luck and success in all your careers. Time for you to *soar* (Figure 10.4)!

Figure 10.4   Small phoenix picture.

References

Aiken, L.N., Havens, D.S., and Sloane, D.M. (2009). The Magnet nursing services recognition program. *Journal of Nursing Administration*, 39(7/8), S5–S14.

American College of Healthcare Executives. (2015). Turnover rates in chief executive officers. American College of Healthcare Executives.

ANCC (American Nurses Credentialing Center). (2014). Magnet application manual. ANCC.

Armknecht-Miller, B. (2014). Looking Inwards: How self-reflection strengthens leaders. *Leadership and Management*. Retrieved from https://www.linkedin.com/pulse/20140910151050-240215-looking-inwards-how-self-reflection-strengthens-leaders/.

Arvey, R.D., Rotundo, M., Johnson, W., Zhang, Z., and McGue, M. (2006). The determinants of leadership role occupancy: Genetic and personality factors. *Leadership Quarterly*, 17, 1–20.

ASN (Aviation Safety Network). (2014). Aviation safety data. Retrieved from http://news.aviation-safety.net/2016/01/01/despite-high-profile-accidents-2015-was-the-safest-year-ever-according-to-asn-data/.

Bandura, A. (1977). Self-efficacy: Toward a unifying theory of behavioral change. *Psychological Review, 84*, 191–215.

Bass, B. (1990). *Bass & Stogdill's Handbook of Leadership: Theory, Research, & Managerial Applications*. New York: Free Press.

Bass, B. (2008). *The Bass Handbook of Leadership: Theory, Research and Managerial Application*. New York: Free Press.

Batcheller, J. (2010). Chief nursing officer turnover: An analysis of the literature. *Nursing Clinics of North America*, 45, 11–31.

Chand, W. (2014). 6 important types of power in leadership. Your Article Library. Retrieved from http://www.yourarticlelibrary.com/business-management/6-important-types-of-power-in-leadership/2560/.

Cherry, K. (2016a). What is democratic leadership? Verywell.com. Retrieved from https://www.verywellmind.com/what-is-democratic-leadership-2795315.

Cherry, K. (2016b). What is autocratic leadership? Retrieved from https://www.verywell.com/what-is-autocratic-leadership-2795314.

Cherry, K. (2016c). What is the ego? Retrieved from https://www.verywell.com/what-is-the-ego-2795167.

Claudian. The phoenix. Retrieved from http://penelope.uchicago.edu/Thayer/E/Roman/Texts/Claudian/Carmina_Minora*27.html.

Clavelle, J., Drenkard, K., Tullai-McGuinnes, S., and Fitzpatrick, J. (2012). Transformational leadership practices of chief nursing officers in Magnet organizations. *Journal of Nursing Administration*, 42(4), 195–201.

Collins, J. (2001). *Good to Great*. New York: Harper Business Review.

Couros, G. (2013). Five characteristics of a change agent. Georgecouros.ca. Retrieved from http://georgecouros.ca/blog/archives/3615.

Cruess, S., and Cruess. R. (2008). Role modeling: Making the most of a powerful teaching strategy. *BMJ*, 336, 718.

Department of Health and Human Services. (2016). Types of doctors and your cancer. Retrieved from http://www.health.nt.gov.au/Cancer_Services/CanNET_NT/Multidisciplinary_Teams/index.aspx.

DePree, M. (1992). *Leadership Jazz*. New York: Random House.

Duperon, S. (2016). Role of celebrity gossip. Dissertation, Wayne State University.

Dvir, T., Eden, D., Avolio, B.J., and Shamir, B. (2002). Impact of transformational leadership on follower development and performance: A field experiment. *Academy of Management Journal*, 45(4), 735–744.

Eder, D., and Enke, J.L. (1991). The structure of gossip: Opportunities and constraints on collective expression among adolescents. *American Sociological Review*, 56, 494–508.

Fischer, B., and Boynton, A. (2005). Virtuoso teams. *Harvard Business Review*. Retrieved from https://hbr.org/2005/07/virtuoso-teams.

Flemming, N. (2001). *Teaching and Learning Styles: VARK Strategies*. Hershey, PA: Idea Group Publishing.

Fogerty, J. (1985). Put me in coach. Retrieved from http://www.azlyrics.com/lyrics/johnfogerty/centerfield.html.

Frankl, V.E. (2006). *Man's Search for Meaning*. Boston: Beacon Press.

French, J.P.R., Jr., and Raven, B. (1960). The bases of social power. In D. Cartwright and A. Zander (eds.), *Group Dynamics* (pp. 607–623). New York: Harper and Row.

Freud, S. (2012). *General Introduction to Psychoanalysis*. London: Wordsworth Classics of World Literature.

Gallup. (2013). State of the American workplace. Retrieved from http://www.gallup.com/services/178514/state-american-workplace.aspx.

Gallup. (2016a). State of the American workplace. Retrieved from http://www.gallup.com/services/178514/state-american-workplace.aspx.

Gallup. (2016b). The engaged workplace. Retrieved from http://www.gallup.com/services/190118/engaged-workplace.aspx?gclid=CLvZpY_J3c8CFQmUaQodL8MGsw.

George, B. (2003). *Authentic Leadership: Rediscovering the Secrets to Lasting Value*. San Francisco: Jossey-Bass.

Gokenbach, V. (2007a). Professional nurse councils: A new model to create excitement and improve value and productivity. *Journal of Nursing Administration*, 37(10), 440–443.

Gokenbach, V. (2007b). *Tap Dancing through Life: 7 Steps to Finding Your Personal Rhythms and the Life of Your Dreams*. Charleston, SC: Advantage Media Group.

Goleman, D. (2006a). *Emotional Intelligence: Why It Can Matter More than IQ*. New York: Bantam Books.

Goleman, D. (2006b). *Social Intelligence: The Revolutionary New Science of Human Relationships*. New York: Bantam Books.

Goleman, D. (2013). Don't write off the coaching leadership style. *Leadership and Management*, August. Retrieved from https://www.linkedin.com/pulse/20130821093435-117825785-don-t-write-off-the-coaching-leadership-style/.

Goleman, D., and Boyatzis, R. (2008). Social intelligence and the biology of leadership. *Harvard Business Review*, 86(9), 74–81.

Greenleaf, R. (1970). What is servant leadership? Retrieved from https://www.greenleaf.org/what-is-servant-leadership/ (accessed April 17, 2017).

Groysberg, B., and Abrahams, R. (2014). Manage your work, manage your life. Retrieved from https://hbr.org/2014/03/manage-your-work-manage-your-life.pdf (accessed April 24, 2017).

Haden, K., and Jenkins, R. (2015). *The 9 Virtues of Exceptional Leaders: Unlocking Your Leadership Potential*. Atlanta, GA: Deeds Publishing.

Hamilton, D. (1998). *Mythology: Timeless Tales of Gods and Heroes*. Boston: Little Brown.

Hay, L. (1996). *Gratitude: A Way of Life*. Carlsbad, CA: Hay House Publishing.

Heathfield, S. (2016). Leadership values and workplace ethics. About.com. Retrieved from http://humanresources.about.com/od/leadership/a/leader_values.htm?utm_term=values%20based%20leadership&utm_content=p1-main-1-title&utm_medium=sem&utm_source=gemini_s&utm_campaign=adid-2dde1ede-5dc5-4e5c-807d-f0865fc84ae7-0-ab_tse_ocode-33092&ad=semD&an=gemini_s&am=exact&q=values%20based%20leadership&o=33092&qsrc=999&l=sem&askid=2dde1ede-5dc5-4e5c-807d-f0865fc84ae7-0-ab_tse.

Henriques, G. (2013). The elements of ego functioning. Retrieved from https://www.psychologytoday.com/blog/theory-knowledge/201306/the-elements-ego-functioning.

Hillman, J. (1996). *The Soul's Code: In Search of Character and Calling*. New York: Warner Books.

Holiday, R. (2016). *Ego Is the Enemy*. New York: Penguin, Random House.

Hollis, N. (2008). *Ten Steps to Authenticity: Creating a Rewarding and Satisfying Life*. Los Angeles: Rhythm of the Drum Publication.

IMPACT Greensboro. (2011). What is a change agent. Impactgreensboro.org. Retrieved from http://www.impactgreensboro.org/what-is-a-change-agent/.

Institute of Medicine. (1999). *To Err Is Human: Building a Safer Health System*. Washington, DC: National Academies Press.

Jeffries, E. (1992). *The Heart of Leadership: How to Inspire, Encourage and Motivate People to Follow You*. Dubuque, IA: Kendall/Hunt Publishing.

Kanter, R.M. (1977). *Men and Women of the Corporation*. New York: Basic Books.

Knaus, B. (2016). All about resilience. *Psychology Today*. Retrieved from https://www.psychologytoday.com/basics/resilience.

Koszyk, S. (2013). The benefits of a multidisciplinary team approach in the health-care industry. Retrieved from http://www.exercisejobs.com/blog/resources/marketing-your-fitness-business/the-benefits-of-a-multidisciplinary-team-approach-in-the-healthcare-industry/.

Kotter, J. (1996). *Leading Change*. Boston: Harvard Business Review Press.

Kotter, J. (2002). *The Heart of Change*. Boston: Harvard Business School.

Kristonis, A. (2004). Comparison of change theories. *International Journal of Scholarly Academic Intellectual Diversity*, 8(1), 1–7.

Kruse, K. (2013). What is authentic leadership? *Forbes*. Retrieved from http://www.forbes.com/sites/kevinkruse/2013/05/12/what-is-authentic-leadership/#5d45d9422ddd.

Kuczmarski, T., and Kuczmarski, S. (1995). *Values-Based Leadership: Rebuilding Employee Commitment, Performance and Productivity*. New York: Prentice Hall.

Leafloor, L. (n.d.) Ancient symbolism of the magical phoenix. Ancient Origins. Retrieved from http://www.ancient-origins.net/myths-legends/ancient-symbolism-magical-phoenix-002020.

Lewin, K., Lippitt, R., and White, R.K. (1939). Patterns of aggressive behavior in experimentally created social climates. *Journal of Social Psychology*, 10, 271–301.

Lippitt, R., Watson, J., and Westley, B. (1958). *The Dynamics of Planned Change*. New York: Harcourt, Brace and World.

Lumby, J., and English, F.W. (2010). *Leadership Is Lunacy*. Thousand Oaks, CA: Corwin Publishing.

Marcec, D. (2018). CEO tenure rates. Equilar Inc., February 12. Retrieved from https://corpgov.law.harvard.edu/tag/executive-turnover/.

Martin, C., and Tulgan, B. (2006). *Managing the Generation Mix: From Urgency to Opportunity*. Amherst, MA: HRD Press.

Merriam-Webster Dictionary. (2016a). Delegation. Retrieved from http://www.merriam-webster.com/dictionary/delegation.

Merriam-Webster Dictionary. (2016b). Innovation. Retrieved from https://www.merriam-webster.com/dictionary/innovation.

Merriam-Webster Dictionary. (2016c). Justice. Retrieved from https://www.merriam-webster.com/dictionary/justice.

Merriam-Webster Dictionary. (2016d). Change. Retrieved from http://www.merriam-webster.com/dictionary/change.

Merriam-Webster Dictionary. (2016e). Humility. Retrieved from http://www.merriam-webster.com/dictionary/humility.

Mizrach, S. (2016). Native American thunderbird. Retrieved from http://www2.fiu.edu/~mizrachs/thunderbird-and-trickster.html.

Myatt, M. (2012). 10 communication secrets of great leaders. *Forbes*. Retrieved from http://www.forbes.com/sites/mikemyatt/2012/04/04/10-communication-secrets-of-great-leaders/#9c8c1b11e06e.

Ovans, A. (2015). What resilience means, and why it matters. *Harvard Business Review*. Retrieved from https://hbr.org/2015/01/what-resilience-means-and-why-it-matters.

Petrilli, L. (2016). How great leaders support work life balance. Lisapetrilli.com. Retrieved from http://www.lisapetrilli.com/2011/08/08/how-great-leaders-support-work-life-balance/.

Phillips, D.T. (1992). *Lincoln on Leadership: Executive Strategies for Tough Times*. Chicago: DTP/Companion Books.

Platske, M. (2016). Visibility and leadership: 7 steps to be the best in your field. Retrieved from http://vivavisibilityblog.com/visibility-and-leadership-7-steps/.

Price, D., and Price, A. (2012). *Introducing Management: A Practical Guide*. London: Icon Books.

Reagin, T. (2016). 10 characteristics of great team leaders. Catalystleader.com. Retrieved from https://catalystleader.com/read/10-characteristics-of-great-team-leaders.

Richards, S. (2015). *Team Leadership: How to Manage Highly Effective Teams*. New York: Berkley Books.

Richert, S.P. (2016). The cardinal virtues: The four hinges of moral life. About.com. Retrieved from http://catholicism.about.com/od/beliefsteachings/tp/Cardinal_Virtues.htm.

Riggio, R. (2014). What is social intelligence? Why does it matter? *Psychology Today*. Retrieved from https://www.psychologytoday.com/blog/cutting-edge-leadership/201407/what-is-social-intelligence-why-does-it-matter.

Sawhney, M., Wolcott, R., and Arroniz, I. (2006). The 12 different ways for companies to innovate. *MIT Sloan Management Review*, 43(3). Retrieved from https://sloanreview.mit.edu/article/the-different-ways-for-companies-to-innovate/.

Schein, E.H. (2010). *Organizational Culture and Leadership*. San Francisco: Jossey-Bass.

Sellman, D. (2011). Professional values and nursing. *Medicine, Health Care, and Philosophy*, 14(2), 203–208.

Semerda, E. (2016). EQ: Emotional intelligence, 3 brain theory and leadership. Retrieved from http://www.theroadtosiliconvalley.com/personal-development/leadership-eq-emotional-intelligence/.

Shirkani, J. (2013). *Ego vs EQ: How Top Leaders Beat 8 Ego Traps with Emotional Intelligence*. Brookline, MA: Bibliomotion Inc.

Sinek, S. (2014). *Leaders Eat Last: Why Some Teams Pull Together and Others Don't*. New York: Penguin Group.

Spence, L., Heather, K., Finegan, J., and Shamian, J. (2001). The impact of workplace empowerment, organizational trust on staff nurses' work satisfaction and organizational commitment. *Health Care Management Review*, 26(3), 7–23.

Sterrett, E. (2014). *Science Behind Emotional Intelligence*. Amherst, MA: HRD Press.

Synectics world, Inc. (2011). Retrieved from http://synecticsworld.com/category/thinking/.

Thach, E., Thompson, K., and Morris, A. (2006). A fresh look at followership: A model for matching followership and leadership styles. Institute of Behavioral and Applied Management. Retrieved from http://www.ibam.com/pubs/jbam/articles/vol7/No3/JBAM_7_3_5_Followership.pdf.

Tuckman, B. (2016). Forming, storming, norming and performing: Understanding the stages of team formation. Mindtools.com. Retrieved from https://www.mindtools.com/pages/article/newLDR_86.htm.

U.S. Consumer Product Safety Commission. (2017). Injury statistics. Retrieved from https://www.cpsc.gov/Research--Statistics/Injury-Statistics/.

U.S. Department of Labor. (2016). Industries at a glance. Retrieved from https://www.bls.gov/iag/tgs/iag31-33.htm#fatalities_injuries_and_illnesses.

Van Vilet, V. (2014). Management and personal development tools for managers. Retrieved from https://www.toolshero.com/.

Van Vilry, V. (2013). Organizational culture model by Edgar Schein. Retrieved from http://www.toolshero.com/leadership/organizational-culture-model-schein.

Wang, Y., and Hajli, N. (2017). Exploring the path to big data analytics success in healthcare. *Journal of Business Research*, 70, 287–299.

Wang, Y., Kung, L., and Byrd, D. (2015). Big data analytics: Understanding its capabilities and potential benefits for healthcare organizations. *Technological Forecasting and Social Change*. Retrieved from http://dx.doi.org/10.1016/j.techfore.2015.12.019.

Winerman, L. (2005). The mind's mirror. *Monitor on Psychology*, 36(9), 48–49.

Index

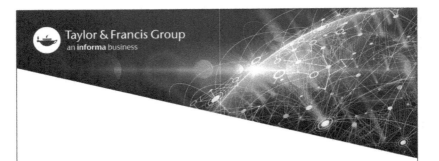